A Guide to Popular Music Reference Books

A Guide to Popular Music Reference Books

An Annotated Bibliography

Gary Haggerty

Music Reference Collection, Number 47
Donald L. Hixon, Series Adviser

Greenwood Press
Westport, Connecticut • London

Library of Congress Cataloging-in-Publication Data

Haggerty, Gary.
    A guide to popular music reference books : an annotated
bibliography / Gary Haggerty.
       p. cm.—(Music reference collection, ISSN 0736–7740 ; no.
47)
    Includes indexes.
    ISBN 0–313–29661–8 (alk. paper)
    1. Reference books—Popular music—Bibliography. 2. Popular
music—Bibliography. I. Title. II. Series.
ML128.P63H34 1995
016.78164—dc20   95–18177

British Library Cataloguing in Publication Data is available.

Library of Congress Catalog Card Number: 95–18177
ISBN: 0–313–29661–8
ISSN: 0736–7740

First published in 1995

Greenwood Press, 88 Post Road West, Westport, CT 06881
An imprint of Greenwood Publishing Group, Inc.

Printed in the United States of America

The paper used in this book complies with the
Permanent Paper Standard issued by the National
Information Standards Organization (Z39.48–1984).

10 9 8 7 6 5 4 3 2 1

I would like to thank A. J. Anderson for supplying the mental and spiritual resouces that have served to inspire, support and motivate my career in information services.

Contents

Preface

This book is intended to be a desk reference. It is modeled after *The Guide to Reference Books* (Sheehy, 1986), but its focus is on popular music styles. The purpose of this book is to (1) help the music reference staff locate books that contain answers to users' questions, (2) direct library users to key resources that can be starting points for larger research projects, and (3) assist acquisition staffs in selecting popular music reference books that are appropriate for their collections.

For the main body of this bibliography, I have only included books that I have personally examined. Unfortunately, since most libraries do not loan their reference material, I could only include items held in collections I could visit. So, even though I have tried to achieve comprehensive coverage, a few minor (but still regrettable) omissions may be found.

A few of the books included in the appendices (those not annotated) I have not examined, but I have confirmed that they are held in major library collections.

Introduction

Subject Areas

Essentially, only sources that are specific to popular music styles are included. General references, such as *The New Grove Dictionary of Music and Musicians* (Sadie), familiar to most librarians, are not covered here. However, some important titles that contain a significant proportion of popular music information, such as *The New Grove Dictionary of American Music* (Hitchcock, Sadie), are included.

Defining Terms

For selection purposes, a reference book is defined as "a book designed by the arrangement and treatment of its subject matter to be consulted for definite items of information rather than be read consecutively." (Heartsill)

For this book, the term *popular music* refers to musical styles that have developed measurable commercial success through recordings and live performance. It is music that was (and is) produced for mass dissemination. Classical or art music is of course excluded.

I have tried to avoid an overly broad historical scope. Jazz, throughout its development, is included, and comprises a significant portion of this book. I have also focused on popular music idioms that have developed concurrently with jazz. Therefore, I have attempted to cover Tin Pan Alley, musical theater, rhythm and blues, rockabilly, and other rock music idioms. Both blues and country music are included because of their link to rock and jazz music idioms and the level of commercial popularity each has attained over the years.

Other folk idioms are excluded unless the focus is on modern popular artists and their music (Bob Dylan, etc.). Gospel music is included because of its commercial success and its influence upon popular music and performers.

Currency
To define practical limits, I have limited this work to include only contemporary and standard resources. Most reference books published over the past few years, that are currently in print, are included. By standard resources I am referring to books that have achieved a history as a reference source. Many are still available (because of a demand) either by the original publisher or as reprints. *The New Encyclopedia of Jazz* (Feather) is a good example. Other standard works may not be in print but are often cited in other works, are still considered viable, and can be found in major reference collections. *Popular Music Periodicals Index* (Tudor, Tudor) is a good example of this.

Breadth
I have tried to include only titles that are comprehensive in their coverage with some deliberate exceptions. The study of popular music revolves around the people who created it, therefore, biographical material comprise a major portion of this book. Many books have been published that contain only a few biographies of popular musicians. Even though these books are undoubtedly valuable for their deeper treatment of the selected artists, their narrow coverage makes them difficult to use as reference sources. As a compromise, I have followed this rule-of-thumb: (1) Biographical collections, in the broad categories of jazz music or rock music, with fewer than 100 entries are not included. (2) Biographical collections, in the narrower categories of popular music (blues music, ragtime, rap, etc.), are generally included no matter how few entries they contain. Biographical collections that focus on a specific instrument (drummers, jazz guitarists, etc.) are also generally included.

Exclusions
I have not included iconography simply because there have been too many published. I have also excluded record price guides. In this age of compact disc reissues, what is a collector's item one day can quickly become just a curiosity the next. Price guides for musical instruments are also excluded.

Citations
Each citation lists the author, title, and full publisher information. Also included is the Library of Congress Card Number (LCCN), International Standard Book Number (ISBN), and the Library of Congress Classification Number when that information is available.

Arrangement
All books are listed in alphabetical order under form. These divisions, typical of music bibliographies, are as follows:

- Only BIBLIOGRAPHIES that are specific to jazz and popular music styles are included. Bibliographies dedicated to a single artist are listed in the appendix.
- INDEXES TO PERIODICALS also include resources that are specific to the musical styles covered, as well as several indexes to magazines that contain significant popular music coverage.
- INDEXES TO PRINTED AND RECORDED MUSIC are mostly song indexes. These differ from discographies in that their focus is on the song, the performer, or performance rather than a specific recording.
- DICTIONARIES AND ENCYCLOPEDIAS are comprehensive collections of information on a subject, style or genre. Books with the words dictionary or encyclopedia in their titles, but containing only biographies, are listed below.
- BIOGRAPHY contains encyclopedic collections of biographical profiles. Books containing interviews or significant quotes are included. Individual biographies are not covered in this book.
- DICTIONARIES OF TERMS include slang, music technology and music business titles.
- DIRECTORIES contain contact information for artists, technicians, music publishers, organizations, recording studios and record labels.
- GENERAL DISCOGRAPHIES are compilations of basic information gathered from record companies.
- CRITICAL DISCOGRAPHIES contain some subjective, usually qualitative, information. Specific discographies of individuals, or individual groups, are listed in the appendix.
- GUIDEBOOKS are travel guides that focus on popular music venues or significant popular music historical sites.
- ALMANACS include list-based fact books AND CHRONOLOGIES include (1) collections of facts listed by the date they occurred and (2) lists of the days of the year and the important facts associated with that day (i.e., what significant things happened on August 1).
- YEARBOOKS are popular music resources that are intended to be published periodically.
- MISCELLANEOUS includes any reference book that does not fit into any of the categories above. Books about music and films or theater, which focus more on the film or show rather than the music, are grouped here.
- APPENDIX A: INDIVIDUAL DISCOGRAPHIES are listed alphabetically by artists and are offered without annotations.
- APPENDIX B: INDIVIDUAL BIBLIOGRAPHIES are also listed alphabetically by artists without annotations.

- APPENDIX C: ELECTRONIC RESOURCES is a list of popular references available on computer discs, CD-ROMs, or by modem.
- The INDEX combines authors' names, titles, and selected subjects. Titles, when listed under an author's name or a subject, may be abbreviated. Each index entry includes the citation number. The subject headings used in the index are derived from the material and are selected from a reference point of view. They are as follows:

AVANT-GARDE JAZZ	MOVIE MUSIC
AWARDS, ACADEMY	MUSICALS
AWARDS, COUNTRY MUSIC	NASHVILLE, TN
AWARDS, DOWN BEAT	NEW AGE MUSIC
AWARDS, GOLD RECORD	NEW ORLEANS, LA
AWARDS, GRAMMY	NEW WAVE MUSIC
AWARDS, TONY	NEW YORK, NY
BANJO PLAYERS	PIANISTS
BASS PLAYERS	PRODUCERS, RECORD
BIG BANDS	PUBLIC DOMAIN MUSIC
BLUES	PUNK ROCK MUSIC
BRANSON, MO	RAGTIME MUSIC
BUSINESS OF MUSIC	RAP MUSIC
COUNTRY MUSIC	RHYTHM AND BLUES
DOO-WOP	ROCKABILLY
DRUMMERS	SINGERS
FOLK MUSIC	ST. LOUIS, MO
GOSPEL MUSIC	SONGWRITERS
GUITARISTS	SOUL MUSIC
HEAVY METAL	TECHNOLOGY AND MUSIC
KEYBOARDISTS	TELEVISION MUSIC
LOS ANGELES, CA	WOMEN MUSICIANS

When possible, review citations are indicated in the square brackets at the end of the annotation. These are from the following journals:

American Reference Books Annual (ARBA)
Booklist (BL)
Choice
Library Journal (LJ)
Notes
Reference Books Bulletin (RBB)
Reference Quarterly (RQ)
Reference Services Review (RSR)
School Library Journal (SLJ)
Wilson Library Bulletin (WLB)

Books Cited in the Preface and Introduction

Feather, Leonard. *New Encyclopedia of Jazz*. New York: Bonanza, 1960. Reprinted by Da Capo 1984.

Heartsill, Young, ed. *The ALA Glossary of Library and Information Science*. Chicago: American Library Association, 1983. p. 188

Hitchcock, H. Whiley and Stanley Sadie, eds. *The New Grove Dictionary of American Music*. London: Macmillan, 1984.

Sadie, Stanley, ed. *The New Grove Dictionary of Music and Musicians*. 6th ed. London: Macmillan, 1980.

Sheehy, Eugene P., ed. *The Guide to Reference Books*. 10th ed. Chicago, American Library Association, 1986.

Tudor, Dean and Nancy Tudor, comps. *Popular Music Periodicals Index*. annual. Metuchen, NJ: Scarecrow, 1974.

A Guide to Popular Music
Reference Books

Bibliographies

1. Allen, Daniel. **Bibliography of Discographies: Volume 2, Jazz.** New York: R.R. Bowker, 1981. LCCN 77-22661. ISBN 0-8352-1342-0. ML156.2.B49

    A listing of discographies published as monographs, in monographs, and in journals. Entries are arranged alphabetically by subject. Most are listed under an artist/ensemble name, others are listed under subjects encompassing: jazz and related styles and idioms; geographic areas; instruments; record companies and executives; and other selected subjects. All of which are listed in the beginning of the book. Blues and early rhythm and blues artists are included. There is a list of all periodicals cited as well as a directory of all small publishers cited. The index combines authors, distinctive titles, and names of series.

2. Booth, Mark W. **American Popular Music: A Reference Guide**. Westport CT: Greenwood, 1983. 212p. LCCN 82-21062. ISBN 0-313-21305-4. ML102.P66B65

    A broad subject bibliography, it is divided into seven sections: (1) American popular music in general; (2) before the 20th century; (3) Tin Pan Alley, dance bands, Broadway and Hollywood; (4) the blues and Black popular music; (5) ragtime and jazz; (6) country and folk music; and (7) rock. Each section begins with brief descriptions of the sources, written in a commentary style, subdivided as necessary. Each section ends with an alphabetically arranged bibliography for that area. Both books and periodicals are indexed, although the focus is on books. There is a general index and appendices. [R: ARBA 1984, pp. 448-9; Notes, June 85, pp. 722-3]

3.   Carner, Gary, comp. **Jazz Performers: An Annotated
        Bibliography of Biographical Materials**. New York:
        Greenwood Press, 1990. 364p. LCCN 90-31765. ISBN 0-313-
        26250-0. ML128.B3C37

        An alphabetically arranged list of jazz artists and ensembles,
        with references to sources of biographical information. The
        sources can be books, theses, dissertations and/or journal arti-
        cles. Entries are briefly annotated and a full, extensive, bibli-
        ography is included. It contains both subject and author
        indexes. [R: ARBA 1991, p. 532; Choice, Dec 90, p. 606;
        Notes, Jun 91, pp. 1161-3]

4.   Cooper, B. Lee. **The Popular Music Handbook: A
        Resource Guide for Teachers, Librarians and Media
        Specialists**. Littleton, CO: Libraries Unlimited, 1984. 415p.
        LCCN 84-19448. ISBN 0-87287-393-5. ML3470.C65

        This education-directed guide to popular music is divided into
        four parts. Part one contains 28 teaching units, each with a
        theme, key terms, teaching strategy and list of resources. Part
        two lists print resources on popular music. This includes: (1)
        bibliographies, divided by musical style, from both periodicals
        and monographs; (2) a selected list of songbooks and lyric
        anthologies; (3) resources on selected popular music topics,
        including more than 100 artists, from both periodicals and
        monographs. Part three lists popular music discographies by
        style (blues, country, etc.), artists and composers, and record
        label. Part four is a recommended popular music record collec-
        tion for libraries. [R: ARBA 1985, p. 487]

5.   Cooper, B. Lee and Wayne S. Haney. **Rockabilly: A
        Bibliographic Resource Guide**. Metuchen, NJ: Scarecrow,
        1990.   352p.   LCCN 90-49760.   ISBN 0-8108-2386-1.
        ML128.R65C66

        An alphabetically arranged listing of Rockabilly artists and
        groups, with bibliographic citations from both periodicals and
        monographs. Many of the periodical sources are British publi-
        cations. It includes a selected discography, a selected list of
        resources, and an author index. [R: ARBA 1992, pp. 535-6;
        Notes, Mar 92, pp. 911-2]

6.   DeLerma, Dominique-René. **Bibliography of Black Music.
        Volume 1, Reference Materials**. Westport, CT: Greenwood,

1981. (Greenwood encyclopedia of Black music) LCCN 80-24681. ISBN 0-313-23140-2. ISSN 0272-0264
———. **Bibliography of Black Music. Volume 2, Afro-American Idioms**. Westport, CT: Greenwood Press, 1981. ISBN 0-313-23144-3
———. **Bibliography of Black Music. Volume 3, Geographical Studies**. Westport, CT: Greenwood Press, 1982. ISBN 0-313-23510-4
———. **Bibliography of Black Music. Volume 4, Theory, Education and Related Studies**. Westport, CT: Greenwood Press, 1984. ISBN 0-313-24229-1. LCCN 80-24681. ML128.B45D44

A comprehensive international bibliography of more than 8,500 book and periodical citations. Most citations are pre-1975.

Volume one focuses on general reference material. It contains 690 citations divided by the broad subject headings: (1) libraries, museums, collections; (2) encyclopedias, lexicons, etymologies; (3) bibliographies of the music; (4) bibliographies of the literature; (5) discographies; (6) iconographies; (7) directories and organization news; (8) dissertations and theses; and (9) periodicals. This volume is not indexed.

Volume two is dedicated to African-American idioms and is divided as follows: (1) general histories; (2) minstrelsy; (3) spirituals and earlier folk music; (4) ragtime; (5) musical theater; (6) concert music; (7) band music; (8) blues; (9) Gospel music; (10) rhythm and blues and other popular music; and (11) jazz. This volume is not indexed.

Volume three is classified by geographic area and begins with a section of general ethnomusicology citations. The main body is divided into four broad areas: (1) Africa, (2) the Caribbean, (3) the Southern Americas, and (4) the Northern Americas. Each broad area is further subdivided into country or, for the North Americas, state or region. There is an index of African culture groups, ethnic groups, languages and regions which links these subjects to the country they are listed under. Contains an index of authors and editors.

Volume four covers the literature on (1) instruments, (2) performance practice, (3) theory, (4) education, (5) interdisciplinary studies and (6) related art, and liturgy. It includes an index of authors, editors and illustrators. [R: ARBA 1082, p. 504; Choice, Nov 81, pp. 354-5; LJ, May 15 1981, p. 1063 (volume 1); ARBA 1983, p. 431; BL, Sept 15 1982, p. 135;

Choice, Apr 82, p. 1045 (volume 2);   ARBA 1983, p. 432;
Choice, Dec 82, p. 554 (volume 3)]

7.   Floyd, Samuel A., Jr. and Marsha J. Reisser. **Black Music
        Biography: An Annotated Bibliography**. White Plains,
        NY: Kraus International, 1987. LCCN 86-27827. ISBN 0-527-
        30158-2. ML128.B3F6

        A bibliography of 147 English language monographs that
        cover the lives of 87 Black artists.   Coverage is broad and
        entries include detailed abstracts.   Birthdates for the artists
        covered range from 1849 to 1959, and artists represent all
        styles of music.   [R: ARBA 1988, p. 505]

8.   Floyd, Samuel A., Jr. and Marsha J. Reisser. **Black Music in
        the United States: An Annotated Bibliography of
        Selected Reference and Research Materials**. Millwood,
        NY: Kraus International, 1983. 234p. LCCN 82-49044. ISBN
        0-527-30164-7. ML128.B45F6

        A "survey of research materials and archives related to black
        American Music" (Introduction). It lists monographs only and
        is not limited to any specific musical style or idiom. It features
        in-depth critical annotations, as well as review sources for
        most entries. It is divided into the subject areas: (1) general
        guides; (2) dictionary catalogs and related sources; (3) bibliog-
        raphies of bibliographies; (4) bibliographies; (5) discographies
        and catalogs of sound recordings; (6) indexes and guides to
        periodic literature; (7) indexes and catalogs of printed and
        recorded music; (8) dictionaries and encyclopedias; (9) general
        Black music histories, (10) chronologies and cultural studies;
        (11) topical studies; (12) collective biographies; (13) iconogra-
        phies; (14) pedagogy; (15) periodicals; (16) anthologies and
        collections of printed music; (17) records and record collec-
        tions; and (18) repositories and archives. It includes an appen-
        dix of general sources, as well as title, author and subject
        indexes.

9.   Gray, John, comp. **Fire Music: A Bibliography of the New
        Jazz, 1959-1990**. Westport, CT: Greenwood Press, 1991.
        515p. (Music Reference Collection, ISSN 0736-7740; no. 31)
        LCCN 91-20601. ISBN 0-313-27892-X. ML128.J3G7

        A bibliography, covering both periodicals and monographs, of

free, or avant-garde jazz music. Entries are arranged alphabetically by artist. These can be subdivided by type - book,
dissertation, article, etc. Entries are also listed under broad
subject and geographical areas. It includes 3 indexes (artist,
subject, and author), as well as a list of artist by country and a
list of artist by instrument. [R: ARBA 1993, p. 544; Choice,
Mar 92, p. 1044; LJ, Mar 1 1992, p. 82]

10.   Gray, Michael H. **Bibliography of Discographies: Volume
       3, Popular Music**. New York: R.R. Bowker, 1983. 205p.
       LCCN 82-20776. ISBN 0-8352-1683-7. ML156.2.B49

A guide to discographies found in periodicals (more than 140
magazines are traced) and individual monographs. The focus
of this volume is on rock music; movie and stage music;
country music; and balladeers and orchestral themes. It is
arranged by subject (mostly artists' names).   Each entry
includes a code indicating which details (personnel, matrix
number, etc.) the discography contains. [R: ARBA 1984, p.
442]

11.   Hanel, Ed, comp. **The Essential Guide to Rock Books**.
       London: Omnibus Press, 1983. 95p. ISBN 0-7119-0109-0.

A bibliography of about 1,000 American and British rock
books. Entries includes title, author, publisher, and a very
brief annotation. Divided into five sections: (1) general reference books (actually not reference books, but general monographs); (2) information books (these are the reference books -
encyclopedias, etc.); (3) picture books, cartoon books; (4)
groups and artists (biographies, discographies, etc.); and (5)
publishers' address list.

12.   Hart, Mary L., Brenda M. Eagles and Lisa Howorth. **The
       Blues: A Bibliographic Guide**. New York: Garland, 1989.
       636p. LCCN 89-34943. ISBN 0-8240-8506-X. ML128.B49H3

An extensive subject bibliography of the blues, its background,
and related subjects. It covers both periodicals and monographs. The text is divided into nine subject areas: (1) background (African-American history and folklore); (2) music of
the blues (transcriptions and studies of blues music); (3)
poetry of the blues (transcriptions and studies of blues lyrics);
(4) blues and society; (5) blues in American literature; (6) biog-

raphies; (7) instruction; (8) blues on film; and (9) research
(methodology and reference). It includes an author index and
a title index (including titles of articles from periodicals). [R:
ARBA 1990, p. 544; Notes, Dec 90, p.387]

13.   Hefele, Bernhard. **Jazz Bibliography**. Munich: K.G. Saur,
       1981. LCCN 81-102540. ISBN 3-598-10205-4. ML128.J3H43

       A bibliography of "international literature on jazz, blues, spir-
       ituals, gospel and ragtime music with a selected list of works
       on the social and cultural background from the beginning to
       the present" (title page). It contains 6,600 citations from both
       books and periodicals divided into 28 subject areas. These
       areas are: periodicals; bibliographies; discographies; reference
       works; background; blues; spirituals and Gospel music;
       general literature on jazz; history of jazz; jazz by country;
       styles of jazz; ragtime; sociology of jazz; the language of jazz;
       the elements of jazz; jazz and other forms of music; jazz in the
       church; didactics of jazz; jazz people - generalities; jazz people
       from A to Z; jazz organizations; jazz clubs; jazz in archives,
       libraries, museums; jazz and TV, radio and film; jazz and
       phonograph records; jazz instruments; jazz and dance; and
       jazz in pictures. Entries are minimally annotated. The intro-
       duction and the table of contents are in both English and
       German. The entries are in the language of the source. It
       includes a name index of both authors and artists. [R: ARBA
       1982, pp. 525-6; Notes, Sept 82, pp. 102-3]

14.   Hoffmann, Frank. **The Literature of Rock, 1954-1978**.
       Metuchen, NJ: Scarecrow, 1981.   337p.   LCCN 80-23459.
       ISBN 0-8108-1371-8.
       ———. **The Literature of Rock II, 1979-1983**. Metuchen, NJ:
       Scarecrow, 1986. 2 v. 1,097p. LCCN 85-8384 ISBN 0-8108-
       1821-3. ML128.R6H6
       ———. **The Literature of Rock, III, 1984-1990**. Metuchen,
       NJ: Scarecrow, 1994. 2 v. 1,008p. ISBN 0-8108-2762-X

       A bibliography of rock music covering both monograph and
       periodical sources. It is divided into 21 subjects, many of
       which are subdivided resulting in a total of 88 headings. It
       includes two appendices: A list of popular music periodicals,
       and a basic list of rock recordings (for the period covered). The
       general index includes: artists, ensembles, subjects, and movie
       titles.
       The second volume is similar in design to the 1981 publica-

tion. It includes book and periodical sources published from 1979 to 1983, along with additional material for 1954-1978. It is still divided into 21 general subjects, though some of these are changed causing differences in the chapter numbers between the editions. The subjects, in this volume, are further subdivided into a total of 112 headings. The entries for books now refer the reader to a numbered reference list (The 1981 volume gave citations each time a book was indexed). Like the first volume it includes a list of journals indexed; a basic list of rock recordings (for the period covered); and an index of artists, ensembles, subjects, and movie titles. [R: ARBA 1982, pp. 526-7; Choice, Nov 81, p. 356; LJ, July 81, p. 1404; WLB, Oct 81, P. 143 (1954-1978). ARBA 1987. p. 495; Choice, Nov 86, p. 454; LJ, Sept 15 1986, p. 78; WLB, Oct 86, p. 67 (1979-1983)]

15. Horn, David. **The Literature of American Music in Books and Folk Music Collections**. Metuchen, NJ: Scarecrow Press, 1977. 556p. LCCN 76-13160. ISBN 0-8108-0996-6
———. **The Literature of American Music in Books and Folk Music Collections, Supplement 1**. Metuchen, NJ: Scarecrow Press, 1988. 586p. LCCN 87-9630. ISBN 0-8108-1997-X. ML120.U5H7

An extensive bibliography on American music. Even though this book is broad in scope, encompassing all styles and genres of American music, about half is dedicated to popular music styles. Three major sections: (1)Black music, which includes gospel, blues, rhythm and blues, and soul music; (2)jazz; and (3)popular currents which includes musicals and rock music, comprise most of the popular music entries. Elumes contains about 1,500 entries with full citations and critical annotations.

16. Iwaschkin, Roman. **Popular Music: A Reference Guide**. New York: Garland, 1986. 658p. LCCN 85-45140. ISBN 0-8240-8680-5. ML128.P63I95

A sparsely annotated bibliography of English language monographs covering all styles of popular music, including jazz. It is divided into seven general areas: the music (subdivided into general and musical styles); biographies (both collective - subdivided into general and styles, and individual - alphabetical by artist/ensemble); technical (education, appreciation, techniques, and instruments); business; product (songs and recording); literary works; and periodicals. More British pub-

lications are included here than in other bibliographies. The
index includes artists/ensembles, authors and a some titles
(for some reason many titles are not indexed). [R: ARBA 1987,
p. 493; Choice, Dec 86, p. 606; LJ, July 86, p. 72]

17.   Jackson, Irene V., comp. **Afro-American Religious Music:
A Bibliography and a Catalogue of Gospel Music**.
Westport, CT: Greenwood Press, 1979.   210 p.   LCCN 78-
60527. ISBN 0-313-20560-4. ML128.S4.J3

Both a bibliography and a catalog of published sheet music of
Gospel Music and spirituals. The bibliography is divided into
six areas including: history and culture, ethnomusicology, folk
songs, spirituals, the Black Church, and the Caribbean.
Citations are listed alphabetically by author within each
section.   The music catalog is arranged by composer and
includes titles, publishers, arrangers and copyright year. It
includes a subject index to the bibliography and a name index
to the catalog.

18.   Kennington, Donald and Danny Read. **The Literature of
Jazz: A Critical Guide**. 2d ed. Chicago: American Library
Association, 1980.   LCCN 80-19837.   ISBN 0-8389-0313-4.
ML128.J3K45 1980

A selective, briefly annotated, bibliography of books on jazz. It
is divided into eight section, each begins with a commentary
on the literature, followed by a bibliography of the titles dis-
cussed. The sections are: general background; the blues; histories; lives of musicians; analysis, theory and criticism; reference sources; education; jazz in literature; and periodicals. It
includes both a name index (both author and artist) and a title
index. [R: ARBA 1982, p. 527; LJ, June 1 1981, p. 1210]

19.   Leyser, Brady J. and Pol Gosset, comps. **Rock Stars/Pop
Stars: A Comprehensive Bibliography, 1955-1994**.
Westport, CT: Greenwood Press, 1994.   LCCN 94-28691.
ML128.R6 L49 1994

A bibliography of monographs about popular music artists and
groups. It contains more than 3,600 citations, arranged alphabetically by name. All listed titles are English-language.
Many are published privately or in limited editions. It contains an author index, a title index and a subject index.

20.   McCoy, Judy.   **Rap Music in the 1980s: A Reference Guide**. Metuchen, NJ: Scarecrow, 1992. 275p. LCCN 92-39684. ISBN 0-8108-2649-6. ML128.R28M3

An annotated bibliography of rap music, listing more than 1,000 articles, books and reviews. The focus is on the music, as well as the artists, culture and politics of the genre. It includes a selective discography of 76 milestone albums, each with historical annotation. It also includes an artist index, a title index, and a subject index, and a date of publication index. [R: ARBA 1994, p. 563; Choice, Dec 93, p. 588; RBB, Oct 15 1993, p. 475; RQ, Fall 1993, p. 133]

21.   Meadows, Eddie S.   **Jazz Reference and Research Materials: A Bibliography**. New York: Garland, 1981. 300p. LCCN 80-8521. ISBN 0-8240-9463-8. ML128.J3M33

A bibliography that "is intended to provide a thorough survey of books, articles, and thesis and dissertations written on or about specific jazz styles and jazz musicians"(introduction). It includes over 2,500 entries and covers works from the turn of the century through 1978. It is divided in two major sections: jazz and its genres; and reference materials. The first section is subdivided into five areas: general; pre-swing; swing; bop; and modern. Each subdivision is further divided by: books; articles; and theses. The second section is divided by: bibliographies-dictionaries-encyclopedias; biographies; discographies; histories-surveys; technical materials (theory, analysis, etc.); anthologies-collections (recordings); and jazz research libraries. Section two is briefly annotated. Each section is individually indexed. [R: ARBA 1982, p. 529; Choice, Mar 82, p. 892; LJ, Dec 15 1981, p. 2382]

22.   Mecklenburg, Carl Gregor Herzog zu.   **International Jazz Bibliography: Jazz Books from 1919 to 1968**. Baden-Baden, Germany: Editions P.H. Heitz, 1969. 198p. LCCN-71-92004
——.   **1970 Supplement to the International Jazz Bibliography**. Graz, Austria: Universal Edition, 1971. LCCN 76-370680
——.   **1971/72/73 Supplement to the International Jazz Bibliography**. Graz, Austria: Universal Edition, 1975. LCCN 75-328480. ML128.J3C4

An alphabetically arranged list (by author) of more than 1,500 books about jazz. Citations are complete and are in the language of the text (mostly English). Nine indexes are included: (1) musicians, singers, band leaders, composers, arrangers; (2) second authors; (3) editors; (4) forward or epilogue and introductory authors; (5) contributors, collaborators, commentators, discographic or bibliographic compilers; (6) translators; (7) illustrators, graphical artists and photographers; (8) country of publication; and (9) subject.

The 1970 supplement lists an additional 429 citations under 14 headings indicating both type of book (bibliographies, reference books, etc.) and subject (blues, rhythm & blues and gospel, etc.). It is not indexed.

The second supplement contains an additional 1,700 citations. It is arranged like the first supplement and includes the additional headings: background literature; beat, rock and pop music; poetry and fiction; and cartoons and drawings.

23.   Merriam, Alan. **A Bibliography of Jazz**. Philadelphia: American Folklore Society, 1954. Reprinted by Da Capo, 1970. 145p. LCCN 75-127282. ISBN 0-306-70036-0. ML128.J3M4

A compilation of more than 3,300 numbered citations; arranged alphabetically by author. It covers both periodicals and monographs. Citations are located using the broad subject index that includes artists and ensemble names. This index refers the user to the appropriate citation numbers. It also includes is a list of periodicals and an index of periodicals entries cited. [R: Notes, Sept 72, pp. 34-8]

24.   Moon, Pete, comp. and Barry Witherden, eds.   **A Bibliography of Jazz Discographies: Published Since 1960**. 3d ed. South Harrow, England: British Institute of Jazz Studies, 1972. 40p. [un-numbered]. ML128.J3M6

An alphabetical (by artist) list of discographies of jazz and blues artists from both periodicals and monographs. Entries include compiler(s), source or format, and annotation. Also listed are collections of discographies, discographies-in-progress, and addresses of discographers. [R: RSR, July 78, p.61]

25.   Reisner, Robert George, comp. **The Literature of Jazz: A Selective Bibliography**. New York: New York Public Library, 1959. 63p. LCCN 59-9577

A selective bibliography in three sections: books (about jazz - including fiction); background books (African-American folk-lore/history, music theory and history, etc.); and selected magazine references. Each section is arranged alphabetically, and there is no index. This is one of the earliest attempts at jazz bibliography. [R: Notes, July 1959, p. 398]

26.   Skowronski, Joann.   **Black Music in America: A Bibliography**.   Metuchen, NJ: Scarecrow, 1981.   723p. LCCN 81-5609.   ISBN 0-8108-1443-9.   ML128.B45S6

A listing of more than 14,000 citations covering both mono-graphs and periodicals.   It is divided into three sections: selected musicians and singers (alphabetical by artist or ensemble - comprises most of the book); general references (chronological arrangement - divided into eight time-periods through 1979); and reference works (bibliographies, discogra-phies, etc.).   It is not annotated and includes an author index only.   [R: ARBA 1983, p. 433; Choice, Apr 82, p. 1050; RQ, Sum 82, pp. 411-2; WLB, Mar 82, 541]

27.   Spradling, Mary Mace.   **In Black and White: A Guide to Magazine Articles, Newspaper Articles, and Books Concerning More Than 15,000 Black Individuals and Groups**. 3d ed. Detroit: Gale Research, 1980. 1282p.
———.   **In Black and White Supplement: A Guide to Magazine Articles, Newspaper Articles, and Books Concerning More Than 6,700 Black Individuals and Groups**. Detroit: Gale Research, 1985. 628p. E185.96.A12S66

Even though this bibliography's scope goes well beyond popular music, it's coverage of musicians and groups is valu-able and extensive.   It is arranged alphabetically by name and includes many citations not found in traditional sources.   A handy occupational index is included. [R: ARBA 1981, p. 218; BL, May 1 1981, p. 1211; Choice, Feb 1981, p. 780; LJ, May 15 1981, p. 1041; WLB, Jan 1981, p. 382]

28.   Taylor, Paul. **Popular Music Since 1955: A Critical Guide to the Literature**. Boston: G.K. Hall, 1985. 533p. LCCN 85-8732. ISBN 0-8161-8784-3. ML128.P63T39

An annotated guide to English language monographs.   It is

divided into eight areas: (1) general works (encyclopedias,
yearbooks, etc.); (2) social aspects; (3) artistic aspects; (4)
music business; (5) forms (soul, reggae, etc.); (6) lives and
works (biographies and discographies); (7) fiction; and (8) periodicals. Most areas, and their subdivisions include an introductory commentary. It includes an author index, a title
index, and a subject (artist/ensemble) index.

29.   Waters, William J. **Music and the Personal Computer: An
       Annotated Bibliography**. Westport, CT: Greenwood Press,
       1989. 175p. (Music Reference Collection, no. 22). LCCN 89-
       23287. ISBN 0-313-26790-1. ML128.C62W37

       A collection of more than 1,300 journal citations arranged
       alphabetically by computer (Apple, Commodore, IBM, etc.).
       Citations come from both computer magazines and technologi-
       cally oriented music magazines (Keyboard, Electronic
       Musician, etc.). [R: ARBA 1990, p. 518]

30.   Wildbihler, Hubert and Sonja Volklein. **The Musical**.
       Munich: K.G. Saur, 1986.   320p.   ISBN 3-598-10635-1.
       ML128.M78W56

       An international annotated bibliography of the literature on
       stage and film musicals. It covers both periodicals and mono-
       graphs published through 1986. It is divided into five general
       sections: (1) general reference works (encyclopedias, year-
       books, etc.); (2) the stage musical (subdivided into 37 subdivi-
       sions including styles and eras); (3) the stage musical outside
       North America (primarily Europe); (4) the film musical; and
       (5) people (performers, composers, directors, choreographers
       and producers). The preface and introduction are in German
       and English, and citations are in the language of the source.
       It includes a list of periodicals consulted, a bibliography, an
       author index, and a subject index.

Indexes to Periodicals

31. Armitage, Andrew D. and Dean Tudor. **Annual Index to Popular Music Record Reviews 1977**. Metuchen, NJ: Scarecrow, 1979. ISBN 0-8108-1217-7
—. **Annual Index to Popular Music Record Reviews 1976**. Metuchen, NJ: Scarecrow, 1977. ISBN 0-8108-1070-0
—. **Annual Index to Popular Music Record Reviews 1975**. Metuchen, NJ: Scarecrow, 1976. 552p. LCCN 73-8909. ISBN 0-8108-0865-X
—. **Annual Index to Popular Music Record Reviews 1974**. Metuchen, NJ: Scarecrow, 1976. 597p. ISBN 0-8108-0934-6
—. **Annual Index to Popular Music Record Reviews 1973**. Metuchen, NJ: Scarecrow, 1974. 681p. ISBN 0-8108-0774-2
—. **Annual Index to Popular Music Record Reviews 1972**. Metuchen, NJ: Scarecrow, 1973. ISBN 0-8108-0636-3. ML156.9.A75

A guide to record reviews published in about seventy popular music periodicals. It is divided into eleven sections according to musical form: rock, country, jazz, blues, etc. Entries are then listed alphabetically by artist/group and include album title, label and catalog number. Review information includes source (an abbreviation of the magazine title), date, page, and number of words. Compilations are also included, listed alphabetically by title, in a separate section. It includes a directory of record labels and an artist index. [R: ARBA 1975 p. 509 (1973 volume); BL Nov 1, 1976, p. 423 (1974 volume); ARBA 1977 p. 469 (1974 & 1975 volumes)]

32.   Clark, Chris and Andy Lineham. **POMPI: Popular Music
        Periodicals Index**. London: The British Library, 1988.
        annual. ISSN 0951-1318.

        An annual index to about 80 (mostly English language)
        popular music periodicals. Entries are listed by subject: per-
        sonal name, group name or subject term. A list of possible
        subject terms, as well as a list of all periodicals covered,
        appear in the front of each volume. [R: Notes, Dec 90, p.390]

33.   Gart, Galen. **First Pressings: Rock History as Chronicled
        in Billboard Magazine**. Milford, NH: Big Nickel, 1986- 89.
        v. I-III (published loose). LCCN 87-123280. ISBN 0-936433-
        00-0. ML3477.F57

        Contents: volume 1, 1948-1950 (1986) 342 p.; volume 2, 1951-
        1952 (1986) 350 p.; volume 3, 1953 (1989) 400 p.
        A chronologically arranged selection of news stories,
        columns and reviews (most excerpted, some adapted) from
        Billboard magazine. Material was selected that chronicled the
        development of rhythm and blues. It includes both an artist
        index and a subject index.
        This series was continued as First Pressings: The History of
        Rhythm & Blues, volume 3 (1953) through volume 7 (1957),
        which is similar to the earlier titles except that all material is
        adapted from unnamed sources. Volumes 1 and 2 were even-
        tually added to complete the newer series.

34.   Gatten, Jeffrey N., comp.   **The Rolling Stone Index:
        Twenty-Five Years of Popular Culture.** Ann Arbor, MI:
        Popular Culture, 1992. 550p. ISBN 1-56075-030-8.

        A comprehensive index covering all published issues through
        1991. Two main indexes (author and title) are followed by
        indexes by: book reviews, concert reviews, movie reviews,
        record reviews, cover art, obituaries, etc. Unique subject head-
        ings are included to strengthen this exhaustive resourse. [R:
        Choice, Sept 93, p. 82]

35.   Lord, Tom. **Tom Lord's Cadence All Years Index 1976-
        1992**. 347p. Redwood, NY: North Country Distributors, 1992.
        LCCN 93-235534. ML156.4.J3L67

        A comprehensive index to Cadence Magazine, containing more

than 30,000 entries, covering 204 issues. The first section is divided into the areas of (1) reviews (videos, books, calenders, and anthologies), (2) articles, (3) columns (Sonics - hi-fi equipt-ment, Chapters in Jazz, The Questionaire); and (4) interviews. The remainder is an in-depth index by artist covering both reviews and articles. [R: ARBA 1994, p. 563; Choice, Apr 1993, p. 1297]

36.   Ruecker, Norbert and Christa Reggentin-Scheidt. **The Jazz Index: Bibliography of Jazz Literature in Periodicals and Collections**. Frankfurt, West Germany: Norbert Ruecker, 1977-. First published quarterly - frequency varied.

An extensive index to international jazz music magazines. Entries are arranged alphabetically by artist/ensemble or selected subject heading. Each entry includes: the title of the article; the auther(s); and the periodical name, volume and page number. It contains a seperate section for articles about the blues. The number of periodicals regularly indexed grew to more than eighty. Entries are both in English and German. The last volume published was #8 (1983).

37.   Southern, Eileen. **The Black Perspective in Music: Ten Year Index, 1973-1982**. Cambria Heights, NY: Foundation for research in the African-American Creative Arts, 1983. 51p.

Although this periodical is not exclusive to popular music forms, it is a major source for scholarly work in the field. It is divided into five sections: (1) authors, titles, subjects, depart-ments and miscellanea; (2) reviews and reviewers; (3) illustra-tions; (4) musical examples; and (5) obituaries.

38.   Tudor, Dean and Nancy Tudor, comps. **Popular Music Periodicals Index, 1973**. Metuchen, NJ: Scarecrow, 1974. 338p. LCCN 74-11578. ISBN 0-8108-0763-7
——. **Popular Music Periodicals Index, 1974**. Metuchen, NJ: Scarecrow, 1975.
——. **Popular Music Periodicals Index, 1975**. Metuchen, NJ: Scarecrow, 1976. 349p. ISBN 0-8108-0927-3.
——. **Popular Music Periodicals Index, 1976**. Metuchen, NJ: Scarecrow, 1977. ISBN 0-8108-1079-4.

A subject index to English language popular music periodicals.

From 47 (in 1973) to 61 (in 1976) peridicals are covered. Articles are listed by subject; most under artist or group, others under genre headings (rockabilly, blues, etc.). Record reviews are not included (see: Armitage & Tudor: Annual Index to PopularMusic Record Reviews). It includes an author index. [R: ARBA 1975, p.511 (1973); ARBA 1977, p. 472; Choice, Jun 76, p. 500; LJ, Nov 15 1976, p. 2360 (1975)]

39.   Vann, Kimberly R. **Black Music in Ebony: An Annotated Guide to the Articles on Music in Ebony Magazine, 1945-1985**. Chicago: Center for Black Music Research, Columbis College, c1990. 119p. LCCN 89-15725. ISBN 0-929911-01-6.

A chronologically arranged list of music related articled from Ebony Magazine. Each entry includes: volume and issue number, title, author, date, beginning page number, and a brief summary of the articles contents. It includes five indexes: authors, (musical) genres, performing medium, subjects, and titles.

Indexes to Printed and Recorded Music

40. American Society of Composers, Authors and Publishers. **ASCAP Index of Performed Compositions**. New York: American Society of Composers, Authors and Publishers, 1978. 1,423p. LCCN 77-95282. ISBN 0-931198-01-1
——. **ASCAP Index of Performed Compositions, Supplement 1981**. New York: American Society of Composers, Authors and Publishers, 1981. 140p. LCCN 81-66118. ISBN 0-931198-02-X. ML120.U5A53

An "alphabetical listing of compositions in the ASCAP repertory which have appeared in the Society's survey of radio, television and wired music performances" (preface) through March 1977. Entries include the song title, the author and the publisher. All styles and forms of music are included. The Supplement lists performed compositions surveyed between June 1977 and September 1980.

41. American Society of Composers, Authors and Publishers. **ASCAP Hit Songs**. New York: American Society of Composers, Authors and Publishers, 1978. 139p. LCCN 78-11329. ML128.S3 A46

A selected list of popular song titles written by ASCAP songwriters. Entries are arranged by title, under the year it was a hit (from 1914 through 1976). Each entry lists the writers. There is an index of song titles.

42. Bell, Malcolm F., comp. **Theme Songs of the Big Band Era**. Memphis, TN: KWD Corporation, 1981. 52p. LCCN 81-141223. ML156.4.B5B44

An alphabetical list of over 850 big band leaders and ensembles. Each entry includes the title of their theme or signature song(s). The record company name and issue number is listed for each song (when available).

43.   Benjamin, Ruth and Arthur Rosenblatt. **Movie Song Catalog: Performers and Supporting Crew for the Songs Sung in 1460 Musical and Nonmusical Films, 1928-1988**. Jefferson, NC: McFarland, 1993. 352p. LCCN 92-56630. ISBN 0-89950-764-6. ML128.M7B46

An exhaustive, alphabetically arranged listing of American and British films. Each entry lists title, vocalists, musical director, composers, lyricists, arrangers, and featured orchestras, instrumental and vocal ensembles. There are three indexes: performer, songwriter and song title. [R: ARBA 1994, p. 537; Choice, Dec 93, p. 580; RBB, Dec 15 1993, p. 778]

44.   Berry, Peter. **"... and the Hits Just Keep on Comin."** Syracuse, NY: Syracuse University Press, 1977. 278p. LCCN 76-48921. ISBN 0-8156-0134-4. ML156.4.P6B47

A guide to the history of popular music. The main body is divided by year from 1955 to 1976. Under each year is a brief overview of music industry events, followed by a list of the top 50 recordings (singles) of the year as selected by the author. This is followed by: (1) a list of Billboard Magazine's number one songs of the year; (2) a list of the most significant artists of the year (selected by the author); (3) the Academy Award (Oscar) winning song of the year; and (4) the NARAS (Grammy) song, record and album of the year. The book includes a selected (though extensive) discography of popular hits (singles) from 1955 to 1976.

45.   Bloom, Ken. **American Song: The Complete Musical Theatre Companion**. New York: Facts on File, 1985. 2 v. LCCN 84-24728 ISBN 0-87196-961-0. ML128.M78B6

An index to nearly 3,300 American musical productions that opened between the years 1900 and 1984. Volume 1 is a list of productions arranged alphabetically by title. Each entry includes: the date the show opened, the number of performances, composers, writers, directors, choreographers, all technicians, and opening cast members. Volume 2 contains three indexes: song titles (more than 42,000); people (more than

58,000 - both talent and technical); and all show titles by year.

46.   Bronson, Fred. **The Billboard Book of Number One Hits**.
       2d. rev. & enl. ed. New York: Billboard/Watson-Guptill, 1992.
       LCCN 92-20318. ISBN 0-8230-8298-9. ML156.4.P6B76

       A chronologically arranged listing, from Rock Around the
       Clock (July 1955) to Save the Best for Last (Feb. 1991), of each
       song that reached the number one position in Billboard maga-
       zine's singles charts. Each entry lists song title, artist, label
       and number, songwriter(s), producer(s), the date that the song
       reached #1, the number of weeks that the song remained at
       #1, and a list of the top 5 songs for the initial week. The
       primary part of each entry is a profile of the artist, along with
       background information on the specific recording, as well as a
       photo of the artist. The table of contents lists all songs,
       divided by year. it includes an artists index and a title index.
       [R: ARBA 1994, p. 557]

47.   Brooks, Elston. **I've Heard Those Songs Before**. New
       York: Morrow/Quill, 1981. 444p. LCCN 80-39725. ISBN 0-
       688-00379-6. ML128.V7B78

       A listing of the top ten songs for each week beginning January
       4, 1930 through December 27, 1980. Compiled from three
       primary sources: Variety magazine (from 1930 to 1935); Your
       Hit Parade (a radio/TV show from 1935 to 1959); and Billboard
       Magazine (from 1959 to 1980). It is important to note that the
       Easy Listening charts, rather than the Hot 100 charts, from
       Billboard were used. The author also included selected songs
       not appearing on the charts. [R: ARBA 1983, p. 446]

48.   Brosta, Joseph. **BPM: A Beats Per Minute Guide to
       Dance Music, 1980-1985**. Northridge, CA: Time Warp Pub.,
       c1986. 212p. LCCN 87-410752. ML156.4.P6B78

       A discography of popular dance club recordings arranged by
       tempo. Entries includes titles, artists and label information.
       Many citations are for club mixes rather than album or com-
       mercial single release. Indexed.

49.   Burton, Jack. **The Blue Book of Broadway Musicals**.
       Watkins Glen, NY: Century House, 1970. LCCN 69-55070.
       ISBN 0-87282-012-2. ML128.M78B87

A comprehensive guide to American musicals, divided by
decade. Each section is arranged alphabetically by composer.
Shows are listed alphabetically under the composer and
include cast, production credits and song titles. It includes an
index of song titles.

50.   Burton, Jack. **The Blue Book of Hollywood Musicals**.
       Watkins Glen, NY: American Life Foundation, 1953. LCCN
       53-6586. ISBN 0-87282-013-0. ML128.M7B8

       A guide to American movie musicals. Films are arranged
       alphabetically by year (1927-1952). Included are movie musi-
       cals as well as films in which "songs play an important part".
       Each film entry includes production company and credits, cast
       and song titles. It includes an index of song titles.

51.   Burton, Jack. **The Blue Book of Tin Pan Alley**. Watkins
       Glen, NY: American Life Foundation, 1962. 2.v. LCCN 64-
       16426. ISBN 0-87282-014-9 (v.1); 0-87282-015-7 (v.2).

       A guide to the music of more than 100 composers of popular
       songs. These are divided into seven chronological chapters.
       The first titled Grass Roots (covering from 1776 to 1890), the
       rest covering each decade to 1950. Lyricists are not given indi-
       vidual entries but are usually covered under the composers
       that they worked most closely associated. It includes an index
       of composers and an index of lyricists.

52.   Chipman, John H., comp. **Index to Top Hit Tunes, 1900-
       1950**.   Boston: Bruce Humphries Publishers, 1962.   249p.
       LCCN 61-11711. ML128.U7C54

       An alphabetically arranged collection of more than 3,000 song
       titles listing songwriters, publisher, copyright date, with an
       occasional brief annotation (who first recorded, who had
       biggest hit, etc.). It covers songs published from 1900 to 1950.
       For a title to be included, more than 100,000 recordings or
       copies of sheet music were sold. A chronological list of the
       song titles is also included. It includes a bibliography.

53.   **Christian Music Directories: Printed Music 1992-93**.
       San Jose, CA: Resource Publications, 1993.

       A comprehensive guide to printed Christian music. It is

divided into four sections: (1) a song index (listing composer(s), year of publication, publisher, and catalog number); (2) a composer index (listing song titles and publishers); (3) a song-book index (listed by book title and including artist/co-mposer/compiler, publisher, catalog number, and all song titles); and (4) a songbook index (listed by catalog number). It also includes a publisher directory.

54.   Cohen-Stratyner, Barbara Naomi. **Popular Music, 1900-1919: An Annotated Guide to American Popular Songs, Including Introductory Essay, Lyricists and Composers Index, Important Performance Index, Chronological Index, and List of Publishers**. Detroit, MI: Gale Research, 1988.   656p.   LCCN 88-21191.   ISBN 0-8103-2595-0. ML120.U5C6

An alphabetical compilation of the most important songs published between 1900 and 1919. Entries include composers/-lyricists, publishing company, first and/or top selling perform-er, and origin of the song. It includes an index of composers/lyricists, an index of important performances, a chronological list of the song titles covered, and a list of publishers with addresses. This is a companion volume to the Shapiro/Pollock Popular Music series.

55.   Cooper, B. Lee and Wayne S. Haney. **Response Recordings: An Answer Song Discography 1950-1990**. Metuchen, NJ: Scarecrow, 1990. 272p. LCCN 90-8728. ISBN 0-8108-2342-X. ML156.4.P6C68

A response recording is one made as a reaction to an earlier recording. It may answer, challenge, comment on or parody another release. This is an alphabetical compilation of song titles with their subsequent response recordings. It includes an index of song titles and an index of performers. [R: ARBA 1991, pp. 525-6]

56.   Cooper, B. Lee.   **A Resource Guide to Themes in Contemporary Song Lyrics, 1950-1985**. Westport, CT: Greenwood Press, 1986. 458p. LCCN 85-21933. ISBN 0-313-24516-9. ML156.4.P6C66

A listing of rock-era songs by social, political and personal subjects, themes or trends. It is divided into 15 areas: (1) characters and personalities; (2) communications media; (3) death; (4) education; (5) marriage, family life, divorce; (6) military conflicts; (7) occupations, materialism, and workplaces; (8) personal relationships, love, and sexuality; (9) political protest and social criticism; (10) poverty and unemployment; (11) race relations; (12) religion; (13) transportation systems; (14) urban life; and (15) youth culture. Each of these divisions is further subdivided into more specific themes. Under each theme is a list of related song titles. Each song title entry includes the recording artist, label and catalog number, and release date. It includes a discography, a bibliography and an index of song titles. [R: ARBA 1987, p. 492; Choice, Sept 6, 1986, p. 138; RBB, Dec 1, 1986, p. 554; WLB, Sept 86, p. 80]

57.   Coryton, Demitri and Joseph Murrells. **Hits of the Sixties: The Million Sellers**. London: Batsford (distributed by McMinnville, OR: Charles T. Bransford), 1992. 287p. LCCN 93-108555. ISBN 0-7134-5851-8. ML156.4.P6C7

A guide to rock/pop music of the 1960s. It is based on Murrell's Million Selling Records, arranged by year (1960 - 1969). Each year begins with a brief overview followed by an alphabetically list of artists and groups that had million selling records. Each artist entry includes a brief biography, as well as the titles and labels of their hit recordings. It includes an index of names and an index of song titles.

58.   Crawford, Richard and Jeffrey Magee. **Jazz Standards on Record, 1900-1942 : A Core Repertory**. Chicago: Center for Black Music Research, Columbia College Chicago, c1992. (CBMR monographs no. 4). LCCN 91-47517. ISBN 0-929911-03-2. ML156.4.J3C7

A listing of songs that have been recorded 20 or more times by jazz performers. Brian Rust's Jazz Records 1897-1942 is the source of information. It is arranged alphabetically by song title (97 in total). Record entries are listed chronologically under each song title. Entries include release date, performer, location label, issue number and matrix number.

59.   Ewen, David. **American Popular Songs: From the Revolutionary War to the Present**. New York: Random House, 1966. 507p. LCCN 66-12843. ML128.N3E9

An alphabetical list of more than 4,000 song titles, most from the 20th century. Each entry includes the composer and lyricist and a brief history of the song. It also lists more than 140 songwriters (with brief biographies) and over 300 motion picture and musical titles (with cross-references to significant songs). [R: BL, Dec 15 1966, p. 428; Choice, Nov 1967, p. 966; LJ, Dec 15 1966, p. 6218; Notes, July 1968, p. 501-2]

60.   Gargan, William and Sue Sharma, eds. **Find That Tune: An Index to Rock, Folk-Rock, Disco & Soul**. New York: Neal-Schuman Publishers, 1984. LCCN 82-22346. ISBN 0-918212-70-7
       ——. **Find That Tune: An Index to Rock, Folk-Rock, Disco & Soul. 2d ed**. [actually, this is volume two] New York: Neal-Schuman Publishers, 1988. ISBN 1-55570-019-5. ML128.R6F56 1984

An index to the contents of 400 song collections (203 and 202 respectively). The focus is on rock music styles. Each volume is arranged in five sections. The first is a numbered list of the collections indexed, arranged alphabetically by title, including publisher information. The second section is an alphabetical index of the song titles (more than 4,000 in each volume) that include songwriters, publisher, copyright date, performers, and the citation number(s). The third section is an alphabetical index of first lines with references to the appropriate song title. The forth section is an index of all composers and lyricists with references to their songs. The last section is a performer index with references to the song titles listed. [R: ARBA 1985, p. 437; Choice Jul-Aug 84, p. 1586; LJ, Mar 1 1984, p. 478; Notes, Dec 84, pp. 286-7; RBB, Dec 1 1984, p. 502; WLB, June 84, pp. 753-4 (original volume); ARBA 1990, p. 548; LJ, Mar 15 1989, p, 66; RBB, June 15 1989, p. 1804; WLB, Apr 89, p. 124 (second volume)]

61.   Goodfellow, William D.   **Wedding Music: An Index to Collections**. Metuchen, NJ: Scarecrow, 1992. 196p. LCCN 92-13745. ISBN 0-8108-2575-9. ML128.W4G6

A cumulated index to 191 sheet music collections devoted to music for the wedding service. The collections are primarily piano/vocal editions, though some are for solo piano or solo organ. The first part of the book is an alphabetically arranged list of full citations for all of the songbooks indexed, each with an assigned reference number. This is followed by the main index which includes both titles and first lines. Entries provide composers' names, instrumentation, and a reference

number for the collection(s) that contains the song. An index
by composer is also included. [R: ARBA 1993, p. 536; RQ,
Winter 92, pp. 287-8; WLB, Oct 92, p. 115]

62.   Goodfellow, William D. **Where's That Tune: An Index to
       Songs in Fakebooks**. Metuchen, NJ: Scarecrow, 1990.
       449p. LCCN 90-20847. ISBN 0-8108-2391-8. ML128.P63G66

       A cumulated index to 64 fake books (more than 13,000 song
       titles). It is arranged in three parts: (1) a bibliography of
       books indexed, each includes publishing information and a
       three-letter reference code; (2) the song title index, with refer-
       ences to the three-letter codes; and (3) an index of songwriters
       with references to their listed song titles. [R: ARBA 1992, pp.
       513-4; Notes, June 1993, pp. 1525-6; RBB, July 91, p. 2071;
       RQ, Spr 92, p. 432]

63.   Green, Jeff, comp. **The Green Book: Songs Classified by
       Subject**. 3d. ed. Smyrna, TN: Professional Desk References,
       1989. LCCN 82-220575. ISBN 0-939735-03-2. ML156.P6G73

       A discography of nearly 20,000 song titles classified under
       more than 500 subjects. The subjects are broad ranged and
       include places, topical subjects (homosexuality, ecology, war,
       etc.), emotions (fear, happiness, etc.), and general subjects
       (from air to world). Songs are listed under the appropriate
       subject, in alphabetical order, along with the artist, album
       title (when available) and label designation.

64.   Green, Stanley. **Broadway Musicals: Show by Show**. New
       York: Hal Leonard, 1994. 4th ed. 372p. LCCN 90-17372.
       ISBN 0-7935-3083-0. ML1711.G735

       A listing of American musicals arranged alphabetically under
       the year that they opened (starting with 1866 through 1992).
       More than 300 entries are included, selected for their signifi-
       cance in the field. Each entry includes: composers, writers,
       producers, directors, choreographers, cast, songs, the name of
       the theater and date of the show's New York opening, the
       number of performances, a plot summary, and any pertinent
       production facts. Most entries also list publisher, performance
       rights, and cast recording information. There are seven
       indexes: show title, composer/lyricist, librettist, director, cho-
       reographer, major cast member, and theater.

65.   Havlice, Patricia Pate. **Popular Song Index**. Metuchen, NJ:
        Scarecrow, 1975. LCCN 75-9896. ISBN 0-8108-0820-X.
        ――. **Popular Song Index, First Supplement**. Metuchen,
        NJ: Scarecrow, 1978. LCCN 77-25219. ISBN 0-8108-1099-9.
        ――.   **Popular   Song   Index,   Second   Supplement**.
        Metuchen, NJ: Scarecrow, 1984. LCCN 83-7692. ISBN 0-
        8108-1642-3.
        ――. **Popular Song Index, Third Supplement**. Metuchen,
        NJ: Scarecrow, 1989. LCCN 89-6414. ISBN 0-8108-2202-4.
        ML128.S3H4

        "A tool for finding words and music to folk songs, pop tunes,
        spirituals, hymns, children's songs, sea chanteys and blues"
        (preface). It is arranged in three sections. The first is a bibli-
        ography of the books indexed, including publisher information
        and an assigned reference number. The second section is an
        index by title, first line of song, and/or first line of chorus.
        (The title entries refer to the citation numbers, while the first
        line entries refer to the song titles.)   The third section is a
        composer/lyricist index that refers to the song titles listed.
        Three-hundred-one song collections are indexed in the main
        volume.   The first supplement indexes an additional 72 song
        collections; the second supplement 156; and the third supple-
        ment 189. [R: ARBA 1976, pp. 490-1; Notes, June 76, p. 781
        (original volume); ARBA 1979, pp. 477-8; LJ, July 78, p. 1386;
        Notes, Sept 78, p. 94; WLB, Sept 78, p. 89 (1st supplement);
        ARBA 1985, pp. 437-8;   WLB, Nov 84, p. 266 (2nd
        supplement); ARBA 1990, P. 540 (3rd supplement)]

66.   Hounsome, Terry. **Rock Record**. 3rd ed. New York: Facts
        on File Publications, 1987.   LCCN 86-29026. ISBN 0-8160-
        1754-9; 0-8160-1755-7(pap). ML156.4.R6H68

        A broad rock discography, intended as a tool for locating rock
        musicians on the recordings that they have appeared upon.
        The first section is an alphabetically arranged list of over
        7,000 recording artists and groups.   Each entry includes a
        complete list of album titles (more than 45,000) with release
        date, label, issue number, country of origin, and a citation
        number. This is followed by an index of all musicians that
        performed on these recordings (about 78,000) with citation
        numbers referring to the artists that they recorded with. [R:
        ARBA 1988, p. 525]

67.   Jacobs, Dick. **Who Wrote That Song?**   White Hall, VA:

Betterway, 1988. 415p. LCCN 88-19351. ISBN 0-55870-108-7; 1-55870-100-1(pap). ML120.U5J23

An alphabetically arranged list of over 12,000 U.S. popular songs. Entries include writers, year of publication, and the name of the artist (or artists) best known for their recording of the song. [R: ARBA 1990, pp. 540-1; Choice, Feb 89, p. 922; LJ, Jan 89, p.79; RBB Mar 1 1989, pp. 1119-20]

68.   Katzmarek, Bob. **Katzmarek's Encyclopedia of Public Domain Music**. Monticello, MN: Katzmarek Publishing, 1992. 53p. LCCN 93-193785.

A guide to songs that are in the public domain. It is divided into 16 categories: (1) general folk; (2) patriotic; (3) children's; (4) Irish; (5) marches; (6) waltzes; (7) polkas; (8) jazz; (9) Broadway; (10) romance; (11) classical; (12) folk/Broadway authors; (13) general Christian; (14) charismatic; (15) spirituals; and (16) Christmas/Easter. Most entries include authors and dates. Songs were selected from published collections so that the music has some history. It includes bibliographies of source material.

69.   Kinkle, Roger D. **The Complete Encyclopedia of Popular Music and Jazz 1900-1950**. New Rochelle, NY: Arlington House, 1974. 4 v. LCCN 74-7109. ISBN 0-87000-229-5. ML102.P66K55

Volume 1 is a chronological listing of popular songs. It is divided by year and subdivided by: (1) Broadway musicals (includes major cast members, composer, lyricist, and length of run); (2) popular Songs (listed alphabetically with songwriter(s)); (3) movie musicals (includes major cast members, composer and lyricist); and (4) representative recordings (the outstanding, typical and/or most popular recordings of the year, divided under popular music and jazz, and listed by recording artist).
    Volumes 2 and 3 contain more than 2,000 brief biographies of musicians and songwriters. These include representative discographies when appropriate.
    Volume 4 contains indexes of performers, movie musicals, Broadway musicals, and song titles. It also includes the numerical catalogs of nine principal record companies as well as Downbeat, Metronome and Academy (music) award winners. [R: ARBA 1975, pp. 510-1; BL, July 15 1975, p.

1200;   Choice, Apr 1975, p. 198;   LJ, Mar 1 1975, p. 467;
Notes, Sept 75, pp. 44-6; WLB, Mar 1975, p. 532]

70.   Kocandrle, Mirek. **The History of Rock and Roll, A
       Selective Discography**. Boston: G.K. Hall, 1988.   297p.
       LCCN 88-21200. ISBN 0-8161-8956-0. ML156.4.R6K64

       A selective list of recordings, divided into 55 categories, then
       subdivided into over 170 headings and subheadings.   These
       headings can be a style or idiom, a geographic area, or a record
       producer.   They are arranged in a chronological fashion with
       artists listed alphabetically under each headings. Both singles
       and LPs are listed with record label and release date.   [R:
       ARBA 1989, p. 493; Notes, Sept 89, pp. 79-80]

71.   Krasker, Tommy and Robert Kimball.   **Catalog of the
       American Musical**. Washington, DC: National Institute for
       Music Theater, 1988.   442p.   LCCN 87-61421.   ISBN 0-
       9618575-0-1. ML128.M78K7

       A guide to the original scores, librettos and books to 75 musi-
       cals of Irving Berlin, George and Ira Gershwin, Cole Porter,
       and Richard Rodgers and Lorenz Hart.   Each show entry
       includes a description of the show, including production infor-
       mation and plot synopsis. Also included are: dates of it's New
       York run, producer(s), director(s), choreographer(s), musical
       director(s), orchestrator(s), and location of original materials.
       All songs included in the show, songs intended for the show,
       and songs later added to the show are examined individually.
       It includes an index of songs.

72.   Lax, Roger & Frederick Smith. **The Great Song Thesaurus**.
       2nd ed. New York: Oxford, 1989. LCCN 88-31269. ISBN 0-19-
       505408-3. ML128.S3L4

       A comprehensive reference that attempts to cover every aspect
       of the literature of popular songs. Over 11,000 songs from the
       16th century to the present are indexed. It covers songs from
       English-speaking countries only and is divided into 10 parts.
       Part I - The Greatest Songs - is a list of popular songs by year.
       Each year includes a brief commentary of music and recording
       industry developments.   Part II - The Award Winners - is
       divided into American and British awards, then subdivided by
       year. Only the major film, theater and recording awards are

listed.   Part III - Themes, Trademarks and Signatures -
includes lists of performers and their theme songs, college
songs, advertising jingles, and political songs.   Part IV -
Elegant Plagiarisms - is an alphabetical list of song titles that
are based on classical, folk, or popular music sources.   Part V -
Song Titles - is an alphabetical list of song titles with lyricists,
composers, dates of popularity and pertinent facts.   Part VI -
British Song Titles - lists song titles (with songwriters) that
were primarily popular in the British Isles. These are divided
by year.   Part VII - Lyricists and Composers - lists over 6,000
writers with their songs that are listed in part V.   Part VIII -
American and British Theatre, Film, Radio and Television -
contains a list of Broadway musicals and a list of movie musicals with release dates and selected song titles.   It also
includes lists of non-musical films and TV/radio shows with
theme songs.   Part IX - Thesaurus of Song Title by Subject,
Keyword and Category - is divided into more than 2300 headings.   Part X - Lyric Key Lines - is a selected list of first lines,
or first lines of choruses, to over 3,000 song titles.   [R: ARBA
1990, p. 541; LJ, Apr 15 1989, p. 70; Notes, Dec 90, pp. 389-
90]

73.   Lewine, Richard and Alfred Simon. **Songs of the Theater: a
       Definitive Index to the Songs of the Musical Stage**. New
       York: Wilson, 1984. 916p. LCCN 84-13068. ISBN 0-8242-
       0706-8. ML128.S3L55

       An alphabetically arranged list of all musical theater songs
       titles from 1925 to 1971 and selective songs from 1900 to 1925
       (more than 12,000 total).   Each entry includes the comp-
       oser/lyricist, the title of the show it is from, and the copyright
       date. The second section is a listing of all musical show pro-
       ductions, alphabetically by title, with opening date; number of
       performances;   composer/lyricists;   songs   in   order   of
       appearance; recording/publishing information; and awards. It
       includes a chronological list of productions and an index of
       composers and lyricists. [R: ARBA 1986, pp. 486-7; BL, Dec 1
       1985, p. 553; Choice, May 85, p. 1306; LJ, Apr 15 1985, p. 66;
       Notes, Dec 86, pp. 301-3; WLB, May 85, p. 626]

74.   Limbacher, James L.   **The Song List: A Guide to
       Contemporary Music from Classical Sources**. Ann Arbor,
       MI: Pierian Press, 1973. LCCN 73-78293. ISBN 0-87650-041-
       6. ML113.L525

       An alphabetical list of song titles based on classical music

sources. Each title includes lyricist/adapter, original composer, and the title of the source work. It also includes a composer index with titles of songs that were derived from their
works.

75.   Lissauer, Robert. **Lissauer's Encyclopedia of Popular
       Music in America: 1888 to the Present**. New York:
       Paragon House, 1991. 1688p. LCCN 90-33935. ISBN 1-55778-
       015-3. ML128.P63L57

       An index of American popular songs from 1888 through 1989.
       About 19,000 songs are listed in alphabetical order. Each cita-
       tion includes title, composer(s), lyricist(s), and date, plus notes
       on recordings or other pertinent facts. It also includes a list of
       song titles by date and a list of song titles by composer or lyri-
       cist. [R: ARBA 1992, p. 529; LJ, June 1 1991, p. 126; RBB,
       Nov 1 1991, p. 568; RD, Sum 91, p. 15]

76.   Macken, Bob, Peter Fornatale and Bill Ayres. **The Rock
       Music Source Book**. New York: Anchor Books, 1980. 644p.
       LCCN 78-1196. ISBN 0-385-14139-4. ML3534.M3

       A selective list of rock songs arranged under more than 70
       personal, social, and political themes (Brotherhood, Drinking,
       Poverty, etc.). Entries include song title, artist, record label,
       and album title (when available). It also includes a recom-
       mended record library, a list of rock films, a list of record
       company addresses, lists of important dates, and a bibliogra-
       phy. [R: ARBA 1982, p. 528; Choice, May 81, p. 1236; WLJ,
       Mar 81, p. 542]

77.   Markewich, Reese. **The New Expanded Bibliography of
       Jazz Compositions Based on the Chord Progressions of
       Standard Tunes**. Pleasantville, NY: Maurice Markewich,
       1974. 45p. ML128.J3M23

       An alphabetically arranged listing of more than 150 standard
       songs, followed by titles of jazz compositions that are based on
       the chord progressions of these standards. Entries, for both
       the standard and the derived songs, include writers, publisher,
       performance rights organization, and selected recording (artist
       and label).

78.   Marsh, Dave. **Merry Christmas, Baby: Holiday Music**

from Bing to Sting. Boston: Little Brown, c1993. LCCN 93-20372. ISBN 0-316-54733-6. ML3470.M355

A survey of Christmas music recorded by popular artists and groups. It is divided into seven chapters; chronologically from the 1940s through the 1980s. It includes a discography of 365 Christmas singles listed by artist. Each entry includes the song title, record label, issue number and year.

79.   Mattfeld, Julius, comp. **Variety Music Cavalcade: 1620-1950**. New York: Prentice-Hall, 1952. 637p. ML128.V7M4

A selective list of popular song titles arranged by year. Each song title entry includes the composer/lyricist, and publisher. Each year includes a brief commentary of important historical, political and musical events. It also includes a list of publishers and an index of song titles.

80.   Miron, Charles. **Rock Gold: All the Hit Charts from 1955 to 1976**. New York: Drake Publishers, 1977. 160p. LCCN 76-43421. ISBN 0-8473-1467-7. ML156.4.P6

A chronological listing of the top 10 rated records from the weekly Record World (British) charts. It covers each month from January 1955 through December 1976.

81.   Murrells, Joseph. **Million Selling Records from the 1900s to the 1980s: An Illustrated Directory**. New York: Arco, 1985. LCCN 84-24218. ISBN 0-668-06459-5
        ———. **The Book of Golden Discs**. London: Barrie & Jenkins, 1978. ISBN 0-214-20480-4. ML156.4.P6M88

A list of every recorded single that sold one million or more units globally from 1903 to 1980 (with appendices for 1981-1982). Artists and groups are listed alphabetically under the year that the record was a hit. Entries include song title, record label and a brief article about the recording and/or artist(s). The original publication, which covered up through 1975 (with appendices for 1976-1977) included 32 pages of various almanac-type tables and three indexes (titles, artist and group, artist theater cast - sound track, etc.). [R: ARBA 1986, p. 484; Choice, Jul/Aug 85, p. 1619; LJ, June 1 1985, p. 116]

82.   **Mus*Key: The Reference Guide of Note**. (Fort Collins, CO: Musi*Key, 1985-). 2 vols. bi-monthly ISSN 0895-1543

A bi-monthly publication intended for sheet music retailers, representing most popular songs in print. One volume contains an alphabetical list of song titles. Under each song title is listed the titles and publishers of collections and folios that contain the song, as well as the publisher of individual sheets. The second volume is in three sections; (1) books (an alphabetically arranged list of sheet music folios by title, including contents), (2) arrangements (collections of songs arranged for a specifis instrument/voice or ensemble), and (3) personality (folios listed alphabetically by artist/group). [R: ARBA 1990, pp. 541-2]

83.   Parish, James Robert and Michael R. Pitts. **The Great Hollywood Musical Pictures**. Metuchen, NJ: Scarecrow, 1992.   816p.   LCCN 92-7483.   ISBN 0-8108-2529-5. PN1995.9.M86P37

An alphabetically arranged listing of about 340 movie musicals. Each entry includes date, studio, running time, production staff, cast, song titles with performer, and an article that includes the story line, film background and criticism.   It includes an index of all film titles covered, arranged by year. [R: RBB, Nov 1 1992, p. 547]

84.   Paymer, Marvin E., ed.   **Facts Behind the Songs**: **A Handbook of American Popular Music from the Nineties to the '90s**. Hamden, CT: Garland, 1993. (Garland Reference Library of the Humanities) 564p. LCCN 93-24342. ISBN 0-824-05240-4. ML102.P66F2

A subject guide to popular songs covering the past 100 years. The first section of this book is an alphabetical list of subject terms followed by brief articles that define the terms and offer example song titles.   Subject terms can be places, musical styles, historical events, record industry terminology, musical styles and genres, as well as general subjects (e.g., Food & Drink, Money, Talking, etc.).   This section also includes 15 tables, including Grammy Awards, singers and their signature songs, etc.   The second section is an alphabetical list of song titles. Each entry includes the composer, the lyricist, release date and performer, as well as all subject terms and tables that the song appears under. It includes a general index. [R:

ARBA 1994, p. 560; Choice, Mar 1994, p. 1094]

85.   Roland, Tom. **The Billboard Book of Number One Country Hits**. New York: Billboard Books/Watson/Guptil, 1991.   584p.   LCCN 90-15588.   ISBN 0-8230-7553-2. ML156.4.C7R64

A year-by-year listing of recordings that reached number one on Billboard magazine's country music singles charts from 1968 through 1989. Each entry includes the song title, artist, writer, producer, the date that the song reached number one, and the number of weeks it stayed at number one. Each entry also includes an article about the song, the recording, and/or the artist. It includes a name index and a song title index. [R: ARBA 1992, p. 532]

86.   Shannon, Bob and John Javna. **Behind the Hits**. New York: Warner Books, 1986. 254p. LCCN 86-15889. ISBN 00-466-38172-1. ML3477.S47

A collection of brief anecdotes (artist's inspirations, record industry politics, etc.) about more than 300 popular songs. The songs are mostly from the 1950s and 1960s, and are arranged by subject.   Most entries, though anecdotal in style, include quotes from the artists, composers or industry personnel involved.   It includes an index of songs titles and an index of artists.

87.   Shapiro, Nat, ed. **Popular Music: An Annotated Index of American Popular Songs. Volume 1, 1950-59**. New York: Adrian Press, 1964.
——. **Popular Music: An Annotated Index of American Popular Songs. Volume 2, 1940-49**. New York: Adrian Press, 1964.
——. **Popular Music: An Annotated Index of American Popular Songs. Volume 3, 1960-64**. New York: Adrian Press, 1964.
——. **Popular Music: An Annotated Index of American Popular Songs. Volume 4, 1930-39**. New York: Adrian Press, 1964.
——. **Popular Music: An Annotated Index of American Popular Songs. Volume 5, 1920-29**. New York: Adrian Press, 1964.
——. **Popular Music: An Annotated Index of American**

Popular Songs. Volume 6, 1965-69. New York: Adrian Press, 1964.

Pollock, Bruce, ed. **Popular Music: An Annotated Index of American Popular Songs. Volume 7: 1970-1974**. 360p. Detroit: Gale Research, 1984. ISBN 0-8103-0845-2

——. **Popular Music: An Annotated Index of American Popular Songs. Volume 8, 1975-1979**. Detroit: Gale Research, 1984. 368p. ISBN 0-8103-0846-0

Shapiro, Nat, and Bruce Pollock, eds. **Popular Music, 1920-1979: An Annotated Index of Over 18, 000 American Popular Songs.... rev. cumulation**. Detroit: Gale Research, 1985. 3v. ISBN 0-8103-0847-9

——. **Popular Music: An Annotated Guide to American Popular Songs.... Volume 9, 1980-1984**. Detroit: Gale Research, 1986. 336p. ISBN 0-8103-0848-7

——. **Popular Music: An Annotated Guide to American Popular Songs.... Volume 10, 1985**. Detroit: Gale Research, 1986. 161p. ISBN 0-8103-0849-5

——. **Popular Music: An Annotated Guide to American Popular Songs.... Volume 11, 1986**. Detroit: Gale Research, 1987. 171p. ISBN 0-8103-1809-1

——. **Popular Music: An Annotated Guide to American Popular Songs.... Volume 12, 1987**. Detroit: Gale Research, 1988. 191p. ISBN 0-8103-1810-5

——. **Popular Music: An Annotated Guide to American Popular Songs.... Volume 13, 1988**. Detroit: Gale Research, 1989. 157p. ISBN 0-8103-4945-0

——. **Popular Music: An Annotated Guide to American Popular Songs.... Volume 14, 1989**. Detroit: Gale Research, 1990. 184p. ISBN 0-8103-4946-9

——. **Popular Music: An Annotated Guide to American Popular Songs.... Volume 15, 1990**. Detroit: Gale Research, 1991. 153p. ISBN 0-8103-4947-7

——. **Popular Music: An Annotated Guide to American Popular Songs.... Volume 16, 1991**. Detroit: Gale Research, 1992. 160p. ISBN 0-8103-7485-4

——. **Popular Music: An Annotated Guide to American Popular Songs.... Volume 17, 1992**. Detroit: Gale Research, 1993. ISBN 0-8103-8234-2

——. **Popular Music: An Annotated Guide to American Popular Songs.... Volume 18, 1993**. Detroit: Gale Research, 1993. ISBN 0-8103-8498-1 ML120.U5S5

A comprehensive guide to the popular songs of the 20th century. Volume one through eight list, alphabetically by title, the most important songs, under the year of original copyright. Entries include composer and lyricist, publisher, first and/or

top selling performer, and origin of the song. Each volume
contains a song title index and a directory of music publishers.
Volumes 1 through 8 have been cumulated into a three volume
set (1920-1079) that combines all song titles alphabetically.

Volume 7 includes a lyricist & composer index which is con-
tinued in all subsequent volumes.

In volume 9, the last multi-year volume, all song titles are
alphabetically grouped together. A chronological index, that
lists all titles under their appropriate year, is included. Also
introduced in volume 9, and continuing through the current
volume, are an awards index and an index of "important performances" (Selected songs are listed under the works in
which they were introduced. These are divided by medium:
album; movie; musical; revue; and television.). [R: ARBA
1986, p. 497 (rev. cumulation)]

88.   Stecheson, Anthony and Anne Stecheson. **The Stecheson
       Classified Song Directory**. Hollywood, CA: The Music
       Industry Press, 1961. 503 p.
       ——. **The Supplement to Stecheson Classified Song
       Directory**. Hollywood, CA: The Music Industry Press, 1978.

       A listing of popular song titles by subject. Almost 400 common
       language categories are used (acrobat, drink, heaven, magic,
       swim, etc.), including selected geographical locations and song-
       writer's names. Song titles are listed alphabetically under
       each subject and usually include publisher. Occasionally,
       songwriters and dates are also included. The supplement lists
       selected popular songs from 1961 to 1978. Approximately 100
       songs are listed for each year and entries include publisher
       and songwriters. Songs are not listed by subject in the supple-
       ment.

89.   Stubblebine, Donald J. **Cinema Sheet Music: A
       Comprehensive Listing of Published Film Music from
       Squa Man (1914) to _Batman_ (1989)**. Jefferson, NC:
       McFarland, 1991. 628p. LCCN 91-52514. ISBN 0-89950-569-
       4. ML128.M7S88

       "The main purpose of this book is to show...which film songs
       were actually published [in sheet music form]" (introduction).
       It is an alphabetically arranged listing of film titles followed
       by the film studio; the release date; the leading stars; song
       title(s); composer and lyricist; publisher; and description of the

cover. It includes a song index and a [selected] composer index. [R: ARBA 1993, pp. 538-9; Choice, May 92, p. 1376]

90.   Suskin, Steven. **Show Tunes: 1902-1985, The Songs, Shows and Careers of Broadway's Major Composers**. New York: Dodd Mead & Co., 1986. LCCN 85-12930. ISBN 0-396-08674-8. ML390.S983

A guide to published songs from Broadway musicals. The focus is on the music of 30 selected composers (with a brief section on selected scores of others). Entries begin with a very brief biography, followed by a comprehensive, chronological list of shows. The information for each show is divided into three parts. The first part is show data including: writers, lyricists, directors, producers, opening date, theater, and number of performances. The second part lists all songs from the production that have been published or recorded. The third part is a commentary, sometimes critical, about the show's music.

91.   Theroux, Gary and Bob Gilbert. **The Top Ten: 1956-Present**. New York: Simon & Schuster, 1982. 302p. LCCN 82-10478. ISBN 0-671-43215-X. ML3477.T5

A guide to the top ten recordings of each year from 1956 through 1981. It is divided annually. Each section begins with an overview of the years music, and includes a list of the top forty songs and a list of the top ten albums. This is followed by one page entries for each of the top ten recordings of that year. Each song entry includes biographical information on the artist (with a photo), as well as background information on the song and/or recording. [R: ARBA 1984, 451]

92.   Townley, Eric. **Tell Your Story: A Dictionary of Jazz and Blues Recordings 1917-1950**. Essex, Eng: Storyville, 1976. 416p.
────. **Tell Your Story No. 2: A Dictionary of Mainstream Jazz and Blues Recordings 1951-1975**. Essex, Eng.: Storyville, 1987. 344p. ML156.4.J3T7

An alphabetically arranged, selected list of approximately 2,700 jazz song titles. Each entry includes the artist's name and record label/number (usually the original, or first, recording) and a brief description or definition of the song title.

Generally, these annotations define terminology (usually slang) or indicate persons, places, etc. that the composer referred to in the title. Volume two is a continuation of the first volume with song titles recorded after 1951.

93.   Tyler, Don. **Hit Parade: An Encyclopedia of the Top Songs of the Jazz, Depression, Swing and Sing Eras**. New York: Morrow/Quill, 1985. 257p. LCCN 85-12375. ISBN 0-688-06149-4. ML102.P66T9

A selective chronology of popular songs from 1920 to 1955. Each entry includes the composer/lyricist and a brief description and history (who sang when, etc.) of the song. Each decade begins with a brief historical commentary. It also includes a selection of brief biographical sketches (artists & songwriters), a song title index and an index of names. [R: ARBA 1987, p. 494]

94.   Voigt, John. **Jazz Music in Print**. 2d ed. Boston: Hornpipe, 1982. 195p. ML128.J3V6

A catalog of commercially available printed jazz music. It consists of an alphabetically arranged list of jazz artists, each followed by an alphabetical list of the published music associated with them. It also includes a list of jazz books in print. [R: Notes, June 76, p. 84 (1st ed.)]

95.   Whitburn, Joel.   **Billboard Pop Charts, 1956-1959**. Menonomee Falls, WI: Record Research, 1992.   LCCN 93-164067. ISBN 0-89820-092-X
——. **Billboard Hot 100 Charts: the Sixties, 1960-1969**. Menonomee Falls, WI: Record Research, 1990. 550p. ISBN 0-89820-074-1
——. **Billboard Hot 100 Charts: the Seventies, 1970-1979**. Menonomee Falls, WI: Record Research, 1990. 560p. ISBN 0-89820-076-8
——. **Billboard Hot 100 Charts: the Eighties, 1980-1989**. Menonomee Falls, WI: Record Research, 1991. 560p. ISBN 0-89820-079-2. ML156.4.P6W443

Reproductions of the pop music singles charts from January 1, 1955 through December 23,1989. The volume first (covering the 1950s) contains several different charts. The Hot 100 charts begin on November 12, 1955 and continue thereafter.

Previous to then are included: Best Sellers in Stores charts (discontinued October 13, 1958), Most Played in Juke Boxes charts (discontinued June 17, 1957), and Most Played by Jockeys (discontinued July 28, 1958). The volumes for the sixties, seventies and eighties contain all of the weekly Hot 100 (pop singles) charts from Billboard magazine organized chronologically. All are reproduced at about 70%. Each volume includes an index of song titles with references to artists and release dates.

96.   White, Adam and Fred Bronson. **The Billboard Book of Number One Rhythm & Blues Hits**. New York: Billboard Books/Watson-Guptill, 1993. 506p. LCCN 93-13336. ISBN 0-8230-8285-7. ML156.4.S6B6

A listing of all recordings that reached number one on the Billboard rhythm & blues (or Black music) charts from 1965 through 1990. Entries are listed chronologically; each includes the title, label/number, writers, producers, date(s) charted at number one, and a brief article about the song, the record and/or the performer. It includes an artist index and a song title index. [R: Notes, Mar 95, pp. 959-61]

97.   White, Adam. **The Billboard Book of Gold & Platinum Records**. New York: Billboard Books/Watson-Guptill, 1990. 308p. LCCN 89-18566. ISBN 0-8230-7547-8. ML156.2.W46

A listing of all recordings that received "gold" and "Platinum" awards from the Record Industry Association of America (RIAA). These awards have been given since 1958 and are based upon record sales. It is arranged alphabetically by artist with recordings (both albums and singles) then listed chronologically. Each entry includes title (A side only), release date, each certification and date (gold, platinum, double platinum, etc.), peak chart position, record label, and issue number. Entries for singles include writers and producers. There are separate sections for original soundtracks, original cast recordings, children's records, and miscellaneous albums. It includes a title index. [R: ARBA 1991, p. 525]

Dictionaries and Encyclopedias

98. Brown, Ashley, ed. **The Marshall Cavendish Illustrated History of Popular Music**. New York: Marshall Cavendish, 1988-90. 21 v. LCCN 88-21076. ISBN 1-85436-015-3. ML3470.M36

A history of American and British pop/rock music from 1955 through 1984. It is primarily made up of brief biographies of rock music's most prominent performers with an occasional subject article. Each biography includes a few record titles for "recommended listening." Each volume is indexed, while all indexes are cumulated in volume 21. [R: ARBA 1991, pp. 527-8; WLB, June 90, p. 148]

99. Carr, Ian, Digby Fairweather and Brian Priestley. **Jazz: The Essential Companion**. London: Grafton, 1988. 562p. ISBN 0-246-13434-8. ML102.J3C321

An alphabetically arranged dictionary containing mostly performers, but also including terminology (musical styles, slang, etc.) and significant geographical areas. It is distinctly contemporary, European and written with a musician's subjectivity.

100. Clarke, Donald, ed. **The Penguin Encyclopedia of Popular Music**. New York: Viking, 1989. 1,378p. LCCN 88-40587. ISBN 0-670-80349-9. ML102.P66P5

An alphabetically arranged listing of nearly 3,000 entries. Most entries are brief biographical sketches of performers and groups. It also includes songwriters, producers, record labels, and musical forms and styles. It covers jazz and blues styles, and also includes some entries for Latin-American, Tex-Mex, Cajun, Zydeco, and African performers. It includes an extensive name index. [R: ARBA 1991, pp. 528-9; Choice, Feb 90, p. 930]

101.   Editors of Country Music Magazine. **The Comprehensive Country Music Encyclopedia**. 1st ed. New York: Times Books, c1994. 449p. LCCN 94-34561. ISBN 0-812-92247-6. ML102.C7 C6

A collection of more than 600 alphabetically arranged entries covering the history of country music. Most entries are biographical although it also includes thematic articles on musical styles, instruments, record labels, venues, and publications significant to the history and influence of American country music.

102.   Gammond, Peter. **The Oxford Companion to Popular Music**. New York: Oxford, 1991. 739p. LCCN 90-14209. ISBN 0-19-311323-6. ML102.P66G35

An alphabetically arranged guide to popular music. American, English and European music is covered, encompassing all styles: jazz, blues, revue, ragtime, popular song, country and western, music hall, operetta, music hall, rhythm and blues, rock, pop, brass, military, and folk. Entries for performers and songwriters are included, as well as descriptions of musical styles, instruments, clubs, impresarios and publishers. Historically, the book's coverage goes back to the mid-19th century, while the focus is on the popular song and musical theater. It includes three indexes: people and groups, shows and films, and songs and albums. [R: ARBA 1992, pp. 529-30; Choice, Oct 91, p. 258; LJ, Feb 15 1991, pp. 184-6; RBB, Apr 1 1991, pp. 1590-1; SLJ, Dec 91, p, 192; WLB, Sept 91, pp. 124-6]

103.   Ganzl, Kurt. **Encyclopedia of the Musical Theatre**. New York: Schirmer, 1994. 2v. (1,610p.) LCCN: 93-48237. ISBN 0-02-871445-8. ML102M88G3

A comprehensive listing of about 2,700 entries encompassing both the productions, and the people, of the musical theater.

More than 1,200 plot summaries are included from U.S. and European productions. Entries for composers, actors, writers, choreographers, directors and producers include a biographical sketch and a list of accomplishments.

104. Green, Stanley. **Encyclopedia of the Musical Film**. New York: Oxford University Press, 1988. 352p. ISBN 0-19-505421-0. PN1995.9.M86G7

An alphabetically arranged reference covering U.S. and British film musicals, as well as selected television musicals. Film title entries list the performers and all songs in the production. Song title entries list the writers, the source film, and a brief description of its place in the film. Entries for individuals (actors, actresses, on-camera musicians, composers, lyricists, directors, choreographers, and producers) include a birth date and place, a brief career profile, and a chronological list of associated productions. It includes a discography of major productions.

105. Green, Stanley. **Encyclopedia of the Musical Theatre**. New York: Dodd, 1976. 488p. LCCN 76-21069. ISBN 0-306-80113-2

A collection of "succinct information regarding the most prominent people, productions and songs of the musical theatre." [preface] It contains an alphabetical listing of show titles (giving cast, song titles, New York and London histories and brief plot summary), personalities (brief information on actors, composers, producers and directors), and song titles (with references to shows, writers, and/or performers). [R: Notes, June 77, pp. 848-9]

106. Hardy, Phil and Dave Laing. **Encyclopedia of Rock**. rev. ed. New York: Schirmer, 1988. 480p. ISBN 0-02-919562-4. ML102.P66H37

An alphabetically arranged listing of over 1,500 brief entries. It includes artists, bands, musical styles and genres, record labels, significant places and historical events. It covers the styles: blues, African and Cajun music, doo-wop, Gospel, new wave, punk and reggae. The perspective is British. [R: ARBA 1990, p. 547; Choice, May 89, p. 1492; Notes, Dec 90, p. 390; RBB, June 15 1989, pp. 1802-3; RQ, Sum 89, pp. 566-7]

107. Herzhaft, Gerard. **Encyclopedia of the Blues**. Translated
      by Brigitte Debord. Fayetteville, AR: University of Arkansas
      Press, 1992. 513p. LCCN 92-7386. ISBN 1-55728-252-8.
      ML102.B6H39

      This blues resource was first published in France in 1979. It
      is primarily biographical but does includes genres, styles,
      instruments and festivals.   Entries include dates, selected
      recordings and a brief sketch of the artist's career. It includes
      a bibliography, an annotated discography, and a list of 300
      classic blues songs with brief history/performers. [R: ARBA
      1994, p. 561; Choice, May 93, p. 1442; RBB, Jan 1 1993, p.
      825]

108. Hischak, Thomas S.   **Stage It with Music: An
      Encyclopedic Guide to the Musical Theatre.** Westport,
      CT: Greenwood Press, c1993. 341p. LCCN 92-35321. ISBN 0-
      313-28708-2. ML102.M88H6

      A listing of musicals and the people responsible for their pro-
      duction. Along with more than 300 shows listed. there are
      entries for directors, choreographers, producers, music direc-
      tors, orchestrators, scenic-costume-lighting designers, actors,
      librettists, lyricists, musical genres, theatre organizations,
      subjects related to the musical theatre and famous musical
      series. It contains more than 900 total entries. It includes an
      index of shows, song titles and persons mentioned within the
      entries. [R: Choice, Dec 1993, p. 586]

109. Hitchcock, H. Whiley and Stanley Sadie, eds. **The New
      Grove Dictionary of American Music**. London: Macmillan,
      1984. 4 v. LCCN 86-404. ISBN 0-943818-36-2. ML101.U6N48

      A very broad, alphabetically arranged, dictionary of the music
      and musicians of the United States. It covers the people,
      places, institutions, instruments, terminology and topics
      which are specific to, or directly related to, American music. It
      does not cover the popular music styles with the depth of the
      subject specific dictionaries, but most major artists are
      covered. Most entries include a bibliography and (when appro-
      priate) a selective discography. [R: ARBA 1988, pp. 510-1;
      Choice, Jan 87, pp. 724-5; Notes, Sept 87, pp. 43-7]

110. Jablonski, Edward. **Encyclopedia of American Music**.

New York: Doubleday, 1981. 629p. LCCN 77-16925. ISBN 0-385-08088-3. ML100.J28

A broad listing of composers, musicians, organizations, musical forms and styles, and terminology related to American music.   Entries are arranged alphabetically within seven chronological sections: 1620-1750; 1750-1800; 1800-1865; 1865-1919; 1920-1929; 1930-1950; 1950-1981.   Each section begins with a brief commentary of the period. All styles of music are represented while entries are brief and coverage is broad. It is indexed. [R: LJ, Nov 1 1982, p. 2127; Notes, Mar 1982, p. 607]

111.   Kernfeld, Barry, ed. **The New Grove Dictionary of Jazz**. London: Macmillan, 1988. 2 v. LCCN 87-25452. ISBN 0-935859-39-X. ML102.J3N48

A very comprehensive resource containing more than 4,500 entries.   It contains biographies of over 3,000 individuals (most with at least one bibliographic citation).   Over 200 musical terms are defined along with surveys of broad topics. It includes entries for musical instruments, record companies and institutions.   It also includes an extensive bibliography. [R: ARBA 1990, pp. 544-5; BL Dec 15 1989, p. 780; Choice, Apr 89, p. 1310; LJ, Feb 1 1989, pp. 61-2; LJ, Apr 15 1989, p. 41; RBB, Apr 15 1989, pp. 1438, 1440; WLB, Feb 89, p. 116]

112.   Larkin, Colin, ed. **The Guinness Encyclopedia of Popular Music**. London: Guinness, 1992. 4 v. LCCN 92-33209. ISBN 1-882267-00-1. ML102.P66G84

A very comprehensive reference book of 3,296 pages (more than 10,000 entries) encompassing all styles of popular music, including jazz. It is primarily biographical, but does include record label histories.   The entries are from 150 to 3,000 words, though some important artists (Beatles, Presley, etc.) have longer entries. Most artists are from the U.S. and the U.K., but many reggae, Latin and Afro-pop artists are also included. Most entries include a discography. [R: ARBA 1994, p. 558; Choice, Mar 93, p. 1112; LJ, Jan 93, p. 98; RBB Feb 15 1993, p. 1080; WLB, Jan 93, p. 108]

113.   Marco, Guy A. **Encyclopedia of Recorded Sound in the United States**. New York: Garland, 1993. 910p. LCCN 93-

18166. ISBN 0-82-04782-6. ML102.S67E5

A listing of persons, record labels, organizations, terms and topics, covering the entire history of recorded sound. Entries range from brief definitions to multiple page essays. The focus is historical rather than current technological. [R: ARBA 1994, p. 539; Choice, Nov 1993, p. 430; LJ, July 93, p. 68]

114.   Panassie, Hughes and Madeleine Gautier. **Guide to Jazz**. Westport,CT: Greenwood Press, 1973. 384p. Reprint of 1956 edition: *Dictionnaire du Jazz*. LCCN 73-435. ISBN 0-8371-6766-3. ML102.J3P33

An alphabetically arranged collection of jazz artists' biographies, songs titles associated with jazz, descriptions of jazz styles, descriptions of instruments associated with jazz, and jazz terminology/slang. It includes a selected list of jazz LPs. [R: BL, Jan 1 1957, p. 220; LJ, Jan 1 1957, p. 86; Notes, July 1957, p. 362; WLB, Jan 1957, p. 283]

115.   Pareles, Jon and Patricia Romanowski, eds. **The Rolling Stone Encyclopedia of Rock & Roll**. New York: Summit, 1983. 615p.   LCCN 83-4791.   ISBN 0-671-43457-8. ML102.R6R64

An alphabetical listing of artists, musical terms and styles, and industry facts. The artists' biographies include birthdates and birthplaces, and album discographies with release dates and record labels. It contains over 1,300 entries and lists Grammy award winners through 1982 (rock artists only).

116.   Peterson, Bernard L. **A Century of Musicals in Black and White: An Encyclopedia of Musical Stage Works by, about, or Involving African Americans**. Westport, CT: Greenwood Press, 1993. 529p. LCCN 92-41976. ISBN 0-313-26657-3. ML102.M88P37

A comprehensive listing of more than 1,200 musical stage works by, about, or involving Black Americans. Shows include musical comedies and plays, vaudeville shows, cabaret shows, and dance revues. Entries are arranged alphabetically by title and can include information on authors, composers, dates, genre, plot, production history and casts. The length of each entry is dependent upon available information and the work's significance. It includes a chronology of listed shows, a name index, a song index and a general index. [R: Choice, Jun 1994, p. 1562]

117. Rose, Al and Edmond Souchon. **New Orleans Jazz: A Family Album**. Baton Rouge: Louisiana State University Press, c1984. 3rd ed. LCCN 84-5721. ISBN 0-8071-1158-1; 0-8071-1173-2 (pbk). ML 3508.8.N48R67

A guide to New Orleans jazz. It includes profiles of artists, jazz bands, brass bands, clubs (both current and historical), and riverboat venues. Entries are very brief. All entries are included in the index.

118. Roxon, Lillian. **Lillian Roxon's Rock Encyclopedia**. Updated and revised by Ed Naha. New York: Grosset & Dunlap, 1978. ISBN 0-448-14571-5; 0-448-14572-3 (pbk). ML102.P66R7

An alphabetical listing of about 300 artists, ensembles, and terms. Most entries are about a page long. Biographical entries include a career history and discography. The discographies are notable for including all tracks for each album listed. Indexed. [R: ARBA 1980. pp. 441-2; LJ, May 15 1970, p. 1975; WLB, Jan 1970, p. 563]

119. Shaw, Arnold. **Dictionary of American Pop/Rock**. New York: Schirmer, 1982. 440p. LCCN 82-50382. ISBN 0-02-872350-3; 0-02-872360-0 (pbk). ML102.P66S5

A collection of over 1,000 alphabetically arranged entries focusing more on terminology and slang in American popular music, than personalities. It includes: definitions of terms and styles; brief biographies of selected musicians and music business personalities; information on pop music landmarks [clubs, recording studios, etc.]; organizations; award winners; nicknames; and slang. It also includes a cross-referenced index of mostly names. [R: ARBA 1984, p. 439; BL, Apr 1 1983, p. 1005; Choice, June 83, p. 1438]

120. Stambler, Irwin. **Encyclopedia of Popular Music**. New York: St. Martins, 1965. 359p. (reprinted by Reprint Services) ISBN 0-685-14819-X. ML102.J3S8

An alphabetical list of more than 380 entries, including performers, songwriters, musical terms, popular song titles, and
musical shows. It includes appendices of Grammy Awards
(1958-64), Academy Awards for music (1936-64), and RIAA
Gold Record Awards (1958-65). It also includes a discography
and bibliography.

121.   Worth, Fred L. **Rock Facts**. New York: Facts on File, 1985.
        416p.   (reprinted by Books on Demand - UMI)   LCCN 85-
        10261. ISBN 0-7837-1363-0 (reprint). ML3534.W65

An alphabetically arranged collection of more than 1,500
entries of unique information about, or related, to rock music.
Most entries are either artist names or song titles, with anecdotal information. The authors intention is to supply information not normally found in books about rock music. Topics and
terms covered are often unique and creative (such as a list of
addresses as song titles). [R: ARBA 1987, p. 496; Choice, Jun
86, p. 1526; RBB, Aug 86, pp. 1675-6; RQ, Sum 86, p. 540;
WLB, May 86, p. 64]

Biography

122. Adler, B. and Janette Beckman, ill. **Rap: Portraits and Lyrics of a Generation of Black Rockers**. New York: St. Martin's, 1991. 106p. LCCN 90-049960. ISBN 0-312-0550-1. ML87 .B36

A collection of brief biographies of about 40 rap artists including excerpts from their lyrics. A heavily illustrated, popular treatment of the subject.

123. Anderson, Robert and Gail North. **Gospel Music Encyclopedia**. New York: Sterling Press, 1979. 320p. LCCN 79-65072. ISBN 0-8069-0174-8. ML102.G6A5

A biographical dictionary of over 170 living gospel music artists and groups. It also includes listings of the Gospel Music Association's Dove Award winners and Gospel Music Hall of Fame members, as well as a discography of major Gospel music recordings. The focus is on country gospel music or inspirational popular music with only a few references to Black religious music.

124. Bane, Michael. **Who's Who in Rock**. New York: Facts on File, 1981. 259p. LCCN 80-20304. ISBN 0-87196-465-1. ML102.R6B36

An alphabetically arranged biographical dictionary of popular music artists from the 1950s, 60s, and 70s. It is written for the non-musician, focusing on the artist's accomplishments and place in rock music history. Entries are brief and intentionally anecdotal. The general index includes names and album titles. [R: ARBA 1982, p. 531; BL Dec 1, 1981, p. 476]

125. Berry, Lemuel, Jr. **Biographical Dictionary of Black Musicians and Music Educators**. Guthrie, OK: Educational Book Publishers, 1978. LCCN 78-62404. ISBN 0-932188-01-X. ML106.U3B56

A collection of brief biographical sketches of black composers, musicians, conductors, educators, publishers, scholars, directors, musicologists and music critics. It includes a name index and a subject index that lists entries by profession (guitarist, publisher, etc.).

126. Bianco, David, comp. and ed. **Who's New Wave in Music: An Illustrated Encyclopedia, 1976-1982 (The First Wave)**. Ann Arbor, MI: Pierian Press, 1985. 430p. (Rock & Roll Reference Series, No. 14) LCCN 84-61228. ISBN 0-87650-173-0. ML12.W5

An alphabetical listing of more than 800 new wave groups. Each entry includes the group's founding date, personnel, chronology (list of accomplishments), articles about the group, record reviews, address, and discography. The second section is a compilation of record companies, each with a list of their new wave recordings. Appendices include a bibliography, a list of magazines and fanzines, and a list of new wave compilation albums. It includes four indexes (personal names, record labels, song and album titles, and geographic location) and a glossary. [R: ARBA 1986, p. 500; Choice, June 85, p. 1481; LJ, Apr 15 1985, p. 75; WLB, May 85, p. 628]

127. Birosik, Patti Jean. **The New Age Record Guide**. New York: Collier, 1990. 288p.
———. **The New Age Music Guide: Profiles and Recordings of 500 Top New Age Musicians**. New York: Collier, 1989. 218p. LCCN 89-9928. ISBN 0-02-041640-7. ML156.4.N48

An alphabetically arranged listing of new age performers and composers. Each entry includes a brief descriptive commentary of the artist and his/her music and a list of record titles with label name. Scattered throughout the book are lists of artists classified under New Age subgenre: (1) electr-

onic/computer music; (2) environmental/nature sounds; (3) folk
music; (4) jazz/fusion; (5) meditation music; (6) Native
American/indigenous; (7) pop music; (8) progressive music; (9)
solo instrumental music; (10) sound health music; (11) space
music; (12) traditional music; (13) vocal music; and (14) world
music. It includes a directory of New Age record labels. [R:
ARBA 1991, pp. 533-4; Choice, June 90, p. 1660]

128.   Britt, Stan. **The Jazz Guitarists**. Poole, England: Blandford
       Press, 1984. 128p. ISBN 0-7137-1511-1. ML399.B74

       A collection of biographical sketches of jazz guitarists. Twelve
       artists are featured and their entries include musical exam-
       ples. The remaining entries are very brief. All entries include
       selective discographies. A brief overview of the jazz guitar
       serves as an introduction. [R: ARBA 1985, p. 433]

129.   Brown, Charles T. **Music U.S.A.: America's Country &
       Western Tradition**. Englewood Cliffs, NJ: Prentice-Hall,
       1986. 215p. LCCN 85-12411. ISBN 0-13-608175-4. ML
       3524.B76

       A biographical dictionary of country artists divided under the
       music's "various stages of evolution" or styles (Western swing,
       honky tonk, rockabilly, etc.). Musical instruments, played by
       country artists, are also described. It includes a selective dis-
       cography, a bibliography and a general index.

130.   Bufwack, Mary A. and Robert K. Oermann. **Finding Her
       Voice: The Saga of Women in Country Music**. New York:
       Crown Publishers, C1993. LCCN 92-44269. ML3524.B83

       A history of the female artist in country music. Although it is
       designed as a text rather than a reference source, it contains a
       great deal of biographical information on artists from the
       1800s to the present time. It also includes full chapters on
       eight significant artists (Kitty Wells, Emmylou Harris, etc.).
       The authors have compiled an extensive bibliography organ-
       ized by artist.

131.   Case, Brian and Stan Britt. **The Harmony Illustrated
       Encyclopedia of Jazz**. 3d ed. revised and updated. New
       York: Harmony Books, 1986. 208p. LCCN 86-15040. ISBN 0-
       517-56442-4; 0-517-56443-2 (pbk.). ML102.J3C34

A collection of brief biographies of jazz musicians. It contains more than 450 entries; most are illustrated with the artist's portrait or album art. Extensive discographies (albums only) are included. It also includes an index of names. [R: ARBA 1988, pp. 523-4]

132.   Charters, Samuel Barklay. **Jazz: New Orleans, 1885-1963, an Index to the Negro Musicians of New Orleans**. New York: Oak Publications, 1963. [reprinted by Da Capo, 1981] 173p. ML3561.J3C43

A collection of brief biographical sketches of more than 950 musicians and groups. Entries are divided into four sections as follows: 1885-1899, 1899-1919, 1919-1931, 1931-. Each section includes a brief historical narrative. It includes a ten page discography/appendix. There are four indexes: (1) names of musicians; (2) names of bands; (3) halls, cabarets, theaters; and (4) tune titles.

133.   Chilton, John. **Who's Who of Jazz: Storyville to Swing Street**. 4th ed. New York: Da Capo, 1985. 375p. LCCN 84-20062.   ISBN   0-306-76271-4;   0-306-80243-0   (pbk). ML106.U3C5

A biographical anthology covering more than 1,000 jazz musicians born before 1920 in the United States. Entries are brief with no discographies. It includes many early blues artists excluded from other jazz dictionaries. [R: ARBA 1986, p. 496; Choice, Oct 1972, p. 953; Notes, July 1973, p. 719; RSR, July 1973, p. 18]

134.   Cianci, Bob. **Rock Drummers of the Sixties**. Milwaukee, WI: Hal Leonard, 1989. 207p. ISBN 0-88188-830-3

A collection of biographies of 14 prominent rock drummers from the 1960s. Written from a drummer's perspective, the entries include some interviews, critical analysis, and musical examples. It also includes a collection of very brief profiles (honorable mentions) of more than 200 drummers from that era.

135.   Claghorn, Charles E. **Biographical Dictionary of Jazz**. Englewood Cliffs, NJ: Prentice-Hall, 1982. 377p. LCCN 82-10409. ISBN 0-13-077966-0. ML390.C59

An alphabetically arranged collection of biographical sketches
of jazz musicians. The coverage is comprehensive, though
entries are very brief. It includes an index of various jazz
groups, listing the personnel. [R: ARBA 1984, p. 452; BL, Dec
15, 1983, p. 611]

136.   Clifford, Mike, consultant. **The Harmony Illustrated
Encyclopedia of Rock**. 7th ed. New York: Harmony Books,
1992.   208p.   LCCN 92-13813.   ISBN 0-517-59078-6.
ML102.R6H37

A richly illustrated, alphabetically arranged, collection of more
than 700 brief biographies of prominent popular music artists
from the 1950s to late 1980s. Each entry includes a selected
discography, listing singles with U.S. and U.K. chart peak
positions, as well as album titles with label and release date.
The book's British origins are sometimes apparent while a
significant number of important artists are relegated to one
sentence in the appendix. [R: ARBA 1994, p. 564]

137.   Coryell, Julie and Laura Friedman. **Jazz-Rock Fusion: The
People, the Music**. New York: Delacorte, 1978. 300p. ISBN
0-7145-2667-3. ML385.C62

Divided by type of instrument, this is a collection of biographical essays and interviews of the fusion performers. [R: BL,
Dec 1 1978, p. 590; LJ, Dec 1 1978, p. 2427; SLJ, Feb 1979, p.
69]

138.   Coupe, Stuart and Glenn A. Baker. **The New Rock 'n' Roll**.
New York: St Martin's, 1983. 192p. LCCN 83-51778. ISBN 0-
312-57210-7. ML102.R6C68

An alphabetical list of rock artists and groups who's careers
began between the years 1977-1983. Entries include a brief
profile with illustration. It primarily covers U.S. and British
groups.

139.   Craig, Warren. **Sweet and Lowdown: America's Popular
Song Writers**. Metuchen, NJ: Scarecrow, 1978. 645p. LCCN
77-20223. ISBN 0-8108-1089-1. ML106.U3C75

A collection of profiles of American composers and lyricists of
popular music. Each entry includes a selected list of the

writer's most successful compositions. The entries are
arranged alphabetically under three divisions: (1) before Tin
Pan Alley; (2) Tin Pan Alley; and (3) after Tin Pan Alley. The
author defines popular music as songs with high record or
sheet music sales. The focus is on song writers who wrote for
musical shows, thus excluding many prominent commercial
songwriters. There is a song title index, an index of productions, and a name index. [R: ARBA 1979, p. 480; LJ Dec 15,
1978, p. 2504; Notes, Dec 79, pp. 372-3]

140. Cross, Colin. **Encyclopedia of British Beat Groups &
Solo Artists of the Sixties**. London: Omnibus Press, 1980.
95p. ISBN 0-86001-638-2. ML394.C76

Alphabetical arrangement of very brief biographies. It
includes many obscure British artists of the period. The index
cross-references musicians with the groups they perform with.

141. Cunningham, Lyn Driggs and Jimmy Jones. **Sweet Hot and
Blue: St. Louis' Musical Heritage**. Jefferson, NC:
McFarland, 1989. 245p. LCCN 88-27353. ISBN 0-89950-302-0.
ML394.C86

A biographical dictionary of musicians born in, or near, St.
Louis, Missouri. It includes 124 musicians arranged alphabetically. Many include a brief interview. Mostly jazz musicians are included though other styles are represented. It
includes a glossary and a general index. [R: ARBA 1990, p.
544; Choice, May 90, p. 1513]

142. Deller, Fred, Alan Cackett and Roy Thompson. **The
Harmony Illustrated Encyclopedia of Country Music**.
3rd ed. New York: Harmony/Crown, 1994. LCCN 93-39779.
ISBN 0-517-88139-X. ML102.C7H37

A collection of brief biographies of more than 450 country
music artists. Entries are arranged alphabetically and include
a selected discography. Most entries also include an illustration. It includes a name index (only listing names appearing
in entries other than their own). [R: ARBA 1988, p. 522;
WLB, Sept 87, p. 93]

143. DiMartino, Dave. **Singer-Songwriters: Pop Music's
Performer-Composers, from A to Zevon**. Billboard Hit

Makers Series   New York: Billboard Books/Watson-Guptill,
1994.   306p.   LCCN 93-44845.   ISBN 0-8230-7629-6.
ML105.D6

A listing of more than 200 singer/songwriters from the 1950s
to the present.   Each entry includes a critical profile and
selected discography.   Selection is based upon commercial
success in the Hot 100 charts, excluding some prominent R&B
and country artists.   It includes an index of artists and song
titles.

144.   Doerschuk, Bob, ed.   **Rock Keyboard**.   New York: Quill,
       1985. 187p. ISBN 0-688-02961-2. ML395.R6

       A collection of profiles and interviews of 24 prominent rock
       keyboardists.   All entries were selected from issues of
       Keyboard Magazine. It includes an index of names.

145.   Eremo, Judie, ed.   **Country Musicians: From the Editors
       of Guitar Player, Keyboard, and Frets Magazine**.
       Cupertino, CA: Grove Press, c1987.   151p.   LCCN 87-011875.
       ISBN 0-8021-3003-8.   ML385.C65

       A collection of articles from Guitar Player, Keyboard, and
       Frets magazines featuring prominent country music musicians
       and groups.   It includes more than 30 profiles and interviews
       originally published between 1976 and 1986.

146.   Eremo, Judie, ed.   **New Age Musicians**.   Milwaukee: Hal
       Leonard, 1989. 111p. ISBN 0-88188-909-1. ML385.N48

       A collection of profiles of, and interviews with, 23 new age
       artists and composers. All were originally published in Guitar
       Player, Keyboard, and Frets magazines between 1984 and
       1988.

147.   Ewen, David.   **American Songwriters**.   New York: H.W.
       Wilson, 1987.   489p.   LCCN 86-24654.   ISBN 0-8242-0744-0.
       ML390.E825

       A collection of 146 biographies of American composers and
       lyricists.   A few songwriters are from as early as the 19th
       century, some are from the 1980s, but most writers were

active from the 1920s to the 1950s. It supersedes both
Popular American Composers (1962) and Popular American
Composers, first supplement (1972). It includes an index of
song titles listed in the entries. [R: ARBA 1988, p. 507;
Choice, June 87, p. 1530]

148.   Feather, Leonard. **New Encyclopedia of Jazz**. New York:
Bonanza, 1960. Reprinted by Da Capo 1984. ISBN 0-306-
80214-7.
——. **Encyclopedia of Jazz in the Sixties**. New York:
Horizon, 1966. Reprinted by Da Capo 1986. LCCN 85-31125.
ISBN 0-306-80263-5.
——.   and Ira Gitler.   **Encyclopedia of Jazz in the
Seventies**. New York: Horizon, 1976. Reprinted by Da Capo
1987. LCCN 87-517. ISBN 0-306-80290-2. ML102.J3F4

The classic biographical dictionary of jazz musicians, it incor-
porates all of the biographies from The Encyclopedia of Jazz
(1955), The Encyclopedic Yearbook of Jazz (1956) and The
New Yearbook of Jazz (1958). Entries are in alphabetical
order and each includes a discography and an address. It is
written with the benefit of the authors' intimate association
with jazz. It includes a list of artists by birthday and by birth-
place.
As a supplement to the original edition, Encyclopedia of
Jazz in the 60s covers all jazz artists who were creatively
active in the 1960s. The biographies for artists listed in the
original volume are updated while new artists are added.
More than 1,100 artists are listed. It includes a directory of
jazz record companies, a selected discography, and a bibliography.
The "70s" edition adds to the series by updating the biographies of artists still active in the 1970s, as well as adding new
artists that have emerged since the earlier volume. More than
1,400 artists are profiled. It includes a directory of colleges
and universities that teach jazz, a selected discography, a bibliography, and a guide to jazz films. [R: ARBA 1988, p. 524;
Choice, July 1967, p. 398; LJ, Feb 15 1967, p. 763 (60s
edition). ARBA 1988, p. 524; Choice, Sept 1977, p. 830; LJ,
Sept 1 1976, p. 1778 (70s edition)]

149.   Flanagan, Bill.   **Written in My Soul: Rock's Great
Songwriters, Elvis Costello, Bob Dylan, Mick Jagger,
Mark Knopfler, Joni Mitchell, Paul Simon, Sting, Pete
Townshend, and Others Talk about Creating Their
Music**. Chicago: Contemporary Books, 1986. 432p. ISBN 0-

8092-5153-1; 0-8092-4650-3 (pbk.). ML3534.F6

A collection of interviews with 29 rock performer/songwriters. Entries are 10 to 15 pages long. The index includes names, song titles, and selected terms. [R: Notes, June 87, pp. 793-4]

150.   Flint, Joseph H. and Judy A. Nelson. **The Insider's Country Music Handbook**. Salt Lake City: Peregrine Smith Books, 1993. LCCN 92-043647. ISBN: 0-87905-563-4. ML102.C7F6

A collection of 275 biographies of country music artists/groups. It includes 800 country music trivia questions and answers and a directory of country music fan clubs. It also includes a day-of-the-year listing (January 1 through December 31) of important events, birthdays and number one songs. It is indexed by personal name.

151.   Fox, Ted. **In the Groove: The People Behind the Music**. New York: St. Martins, 1986. 361p. LCCN 86-13812. ISBN 0-312-41166-9. ML3477.F7

A collection of detailed interviews with 12 influential music industry personalities. Each has made important contributions to popular music as a record company executive, record producer, and/or songwriter. The index includes names (personal and record company) and song titles. [R: Notes, June 87, pp. 793-4]

152.   Futrell, Jon, et al. **The Illustrated Encyclopedia of Black Music**. New York: Harmony, 1982. 224p. LCCN 82-3090. ISBN 0-517-54779-7. ML106.U3G54

A collection of brief biographies of more than 650 soul, funk, reggae, rhythm and blues, disco and jazz-funk artists and groups. Jazz musicians are not included. Entries are arranged alphabetically by decade (The 40s & 50s; The 60s; The 70s) with selective discographies. Most entries include an illustration. A name index is included. [R: ARBA 1984, pp. 437-8; LJ Apr 15 1983, p. 816]

153.   Gentry, Linnell. **A History and Encyclopedia of Country, Western, and Gospel Music**. Irvine, CA: Reprint Services, 1988. 380p. [reprint of 1961 edition] LCCN 71-166231. ISBN 0-403-01358-5. ML200.G4

An alphabetically arranged collection of more than 300 biographies of country and gospel artists. It also includes reprints of 37 magazine articles, about country and gospel music, published from 1904 to 1958, as well as profiles of country music radio shows since 1924.

154.   Govenar, Alan B. **Meeting the Blues**. Dallas, TX: Taylor, 1988.   239p.   LCCN 88-13980.   ISBN 0-87833-623-0. ML3521.G68

Divided by geographic area (Houston, Austin, etc.) this is a collection of brief profiles and interviews of blues artists who were born, or have roots in Texas. It includes a name index and a selected discography.

155.   Grattan, Virginia L. **American Women Songwriters: A Biographical Dictionary**. Westport, CT: Greenwood Press, 1993.   279p.   LCCN 92-32211.   ISBN 0-313-28510-1. ML106.U3G73

A collection of brief biographical profiles (most about one page) of women songwriters and lyricists. 184 American-born artists are included, each with selective lists of compositions. It is indexed. [R: ARBA 1994, p. 543; Choice, Nov 93, p. 432; LJ, Mar 15 1993, p.68; RBB, Jul 1993, p. 2000; RQ, 93, p. 279]

156.   Gregory, Hugh. **Soul Music A-Z**. London: Blandford Press (New York: Sterling), 1992.   288p.   ISBN 0-7139-2179-0; 0-7139-2183-9 (pbk.).

A collection of brief profiles of nearly 600 soul music performers, songwriters and producers. Entries are listed alphabetically and include selective discographies. Soul music is defined as a style which reflects both rhythm and blues and gospel music. [R: ARBA 1993, p. 546; Choice, Oct 92, p. 272; RBB, Sept 1 1992, p. 91]

157.   **The Guitar Player Book**. revised and updated 3rd edition. Cupertino, CA: Guitar Player Books, 1983. 403p. LCCN 83-081371. ISBN 0-394-62490-4. ML1015.G9G84

Profiles and interviews of nearly 70 guitarists representing a broad range of styles (classical, jazz, etc.). It also includes articles about purchasing and maintaining guitars, as well as articles about specific instruments and accessories. All material was originally published in Guitar Player Magazine. It includes a glossary, a directory of guitar manufacturers, and a general index.

158. Hale, Mark. **Headbangers: The Worldwide Megabook of Heavy Metal Bands**. Ann Arbor, MI: Popular Culture Ink, 1993. 542p. LCCN 92-81112. ISBN 1-56075-029-4

An international guide to Heavy Metal artists and bands. It includes nearly 3,500 alphabetically arranged entries. Entries list place of origin, personnel, awards, and a discography. More prominent artists/groups include brief descriptions of live performance. It includes seven indexes (1) band names, (2) performer names, (3) country of origin, (4) U.S. State, (5) band styles and influences, (6) album titles, and (7) album labels & numbers. [R: ARBA 1994, p. 564; RBB, Aug 1993, p. 2090; WLB, May 1993, p. 119]

159. Handy, D. Antoinette. **Black Women in American Bands and Orchestras**. Metuchen, NJ: Scarecrow, 1981. 319p. LCCN 80-19380. ISBN 0-8108-1346-7. ML82.H36

An historical survey of women instrumentalists of all styles of music. It begins with a history of the American orchestra. It is then divided into the chapters: (1) orchestras and orchestra leaders, (2) string players, (3) wind and percussion players, (4) keyboard players, (5) administrators, and (6) the younger generation. Each chapter begins with a historical overview, followed by profiles of individual musicians. It includes a bibliography and a general index. [R: ARBA 1982, p. 532; Choice, May 81, p. 1275; RQ Spring 81, p. 306; WLB, May 81, p. 699]

160. Hannusch, Jeff. **I Hear You Knockin': The Sound of New Orleans Rhythm and Blues**. Ville Platte, LA: Swallow Publications, 1985. 374p. LCCN 84-51112. ISBN 0-9614245-0-8. ML3521.H36

A collection of 26 biographies of notable New Orleans rhythm & blues performers, as well as biographies of 5 important record industry personalities. It includes selective discographies.

161. Hardy, Phil and Dave Laing. **The Faber Companion to 20th-Century Popular Music**. Winchester, MA: Faber and Faber, 1990. 875p. ISBN 0-571-13837-3

An alphabetically arranged collection of more than 2,000 profiles of individuals associated with popular music styles. Most entries are performers, but record producers, arrangers, songwriters, and record industry executives are also included. All styles of popular music are represented, including jazz. Discographic information is included within the text and cross-referencing is extensive. The focus is Anglo-American, with a considerable number of British artists that may seem obscure to U.S. users. An informative, three page, glossary of styles and genres is included. [R: ARBA 1991, pp. 526-7]

162. Harris, Craig. **The New Folk Music**. Crown Point, IN: White Cliffs, 1991. LCCN 90-44717. ISBN 0-941677-27-3. ML87.H243

A slim volume of brief biographies of about 100 folk music artists. It is divided into eight areas: (1) old school, (2) singer-songwriters, (3) bluegrass, (4) blues, (5) Louisiana (6) British Isles, (7) new instrumentalists, and (8) world music. It includes selected discographies.

163. Harris, Sheldon. **Blues Who's Who: A Biographical Dictionary of Blues Singers**. New Rochelle, NY: Arlington House, 1979. Reprinted by Da Capo, 1991. 775p. LCCN 78-27073. ISBN 0-306-80155-8. ML102.B6H3

A collection of 571 biographies of blues musicians, each entry featuring the artist's principle influences. It includes an index of more than 6,800 song titles written by the artists covered, and an index of all personal names and discernible places cited in the text. It also includes a film, a radio, a television, and a theater index listing appearances of blues artists in those mediums. There is a bibliography but no discography. [R: ARBA 1980, pp. 447-8; Choice, July 1980, p. 518; LJ, July 79, pp. 1441-4; Notes, Dec 80, pp.327-8; RSR, Apr 1981, p. 38; WLB, Feb 1980, p. 398]

164. Helander, Brock. **The Rock Who's Who: A Biographical Dictionary and Critical Discography**. New York:

Schirmer, 1982. LCCN 82-80804. ISBN 0-02-871250-1; 0-02-
871920-4 (pbk). ML102.R6H5

A alphabetically arranged collection of biographies of about
300 artists and groups. The entries tend to be critical (rather
than purely historical) and each includes a full discography of
LP recordings.   It includes an index that cross-references
artists and groups and a bibliography. [R: ARBA 1984, pp.
453-4; WLB, Feb 83, p. 524]

165.   Hemming, Roy and David Hajdu.   **Discovering Great
Singers of Classic Pop: A New Listener's Guide to the
Sounds and Lives of the Top Performers and Their
Recordings, Movies, and Videos**. New York: Newmarket
Press, 1991. 295p. LCCN 90-27452. ISBN 1-55704-072-9.
ML400.H43

A collection of 51 biographies of prominent singers who primarily sang "standard pop" songs. These are songs that are
not rock or jazz - many from musical shows. A few included
artists, though, are definitely jazz singers. Entries range from
1 to 10 pages and are divided into two sections; pre and post
World War II. There is a separate section of selected discographies and videographies for each artist profiled. It includes a
bibliography and a general index. [R: BL, Feb 1 1992, pp.
1053-4]

166.   Hildebrand, Lee. **Stars of Soul and Rhythm & Blues: Top
Recording Artists and Showstopping Performers, from
Memphis and Motown to Now**. New York: Billboard Books,
1994. LCCN 94-27594. ML102.S65 H55

A collection of biographies of 180 soul and Rhythm and blues
artists, from the blues shouters of the 1950s to the present.
All artists and groups covered had recordings charted in
Billboard magazine's rhythm & blues/soul/black music charts.
Each includes a selected discography that includes titles and
labels. The index lists names, album titles and song titles.

167.   Hischak, Thomas S.   **Word Crazy: Broadway Lyricists
from Cohan to Sondheim**. Westport, CT: Praeger, 1991.
241p. LCCN 90-47330. ISBN 0-275-93849-2. PN309.L8H5

A collection of biographies of Broadway lyricists, arranged in chronological order. The author focuses on 21 of the most prominent writers, but also includes brief sketches for 56 others. It includes an index of names and titles. [R: Choice, Nov 91, p. 456]

168.   Hood, Phil, ed. **Artists of American Folk Music: The Legends of Traditional Folk, the Stars of the Sixties, the Virtuosi of New Acoustic Music**. New York: William Morrow, 1986.   LCCN 85-63796.   ISBN 0-688-05916-3. ML102.F66A77

A collection of profiles and interviews of 30 major folk musicians and groups. Entries are reprinted from Guitar Player Magazine and Frets magazine. Each entry includes a selected discography and an artist index is included. [R: ARBA 1987, pp. 492-3; BL, June 15 1986, p. 1490; Notes, Sept 86, p. 52]

169.   Jancik, Wayne. **The Billboard Book of One-Hit Wonders**. New York, Billboard Books/Watson-Guptill, 1990.   420p. LCCN 90-844. ISBN 0-8230-7530-3. ML394.J36

A biographical dictionary of artists and groups who have had a recording appear in the top 20 of the Billboard charts, but little subsequent professional success. It is arranged chronologically from January 1955 to November 1984. It includes both a song and an artist index. [R: ARBA 1991. p. 535]

170.   Jasper, Tony and Derek Oliver. **The International Encyclopedia of Hard Rock and Heavy Metal**. New York: Facts on File, 1983. LCCN 84-10236. ISBN 0-8160-1100-1; 0-8160-1133-8 (pbk.). ML102.R6J37

An alphabetically arranged international listing of more than 1,500 bands. Entries include: place of origin; personnel; discography; and a brief critical overview. Only band names are listed - the names of individual musicians are not listed or indexed. [R: ARBA 1986, P. 504; Choice, Sept 85, pp. 82-4]

171.   Kienzle, Rich. **Great Guitarists**. New York: Facts on File, 1985.   246p. LCCN 83-16609. ISBN 0-8160-1029-3; 0-8106-1033-1 (pbk.). ML399.K53

A collection of more than 60 biographies of guitarists. Entries are divided into four areas: blues, country music, jazz, and rock. Entries are from 3 to 6 pages long (most about 4 pages). Some entries are designated secondary essays and are only about one page long. All entries include a selected discography, and it includes an index of names. [R: ARBA 1987, p. 486; SLJ, Apr 86, p. 107]

172.   Kingsbury, Kenn, ed. **Kingsbury's Who's Who in Country & Western Music**. Culver City, CA: Black Stallion Country Press, 1981. 304p. LCCN 81-180447. ML385.W39

A biographical dictionary of country music artists and industry personalities associated with country recordings on charts and play lists during 1979-1980. It contains more than 700 brief profiles of recording artists, studio musicians, disc jockeys, songwriters, record producers, and agents. It also includes directories for radio stations that program country music, country music publishers, record companies and talent agencies.

173.   Korall, Burt. **Drummin' Men: The Heartbeat of Jazz, the Swing Years**. New York: Schirmer/Macmillan, 1990. 381p. LCCN 89-10918. ISBN 0-02-872000-8. ML399.K66

A collection of biographical profiles of 14 jazz drummers. Each entry contains quotations from people "who knew the drummers, taught them, worked with them, [and/or] employed them" (preface). more than 170 sources are listed. Half of the artists are featured with entries averaging about 40 pages, while the remaining artists have entries 2 or 3 pages long. It includes a bibliography, selective discography, and an index.

174.   Kozinn, Allan, et al. **The Guitar: The History, the Music, the Players**. New York: William Morrow, 1984. 208p. LCCN 83-62355. ISBN 0-688-01973-0. ML1015.G9G845

A collection of brief career profiles of prominent guitarists. It is divided into five sections: (1) classical guitar, (2) birth of the blues, (3) jazz-guitar like a horn, (4) country pickin', and (5) rock-kick out the jams. Each section includes background/historical information on the styles, idioms and instruments. The artist entries tend to be more critical than biographical. It includes an index of all names that appear in the text.

175. LaBlanc, Michael L., ed. **Contemporary Musicians: Profiles of the People in Music**. Detroit: Gale Research, 1989-. vol. 1-10. semi-annual ISSN 1044-2197

An on-going encyclopedia of musicians who create or influence the music of today. Each volume offers biographic information on 80 to 100 musicians from all musical styles, though only very popular classical artists are included. It includes artists from the 1950s to the present. Entries are two to three pages long with photo, selected discographies and bibliographic sources. Each volume includes a cumulated artist index and a cumulated subject (style, genre, instrument, occupation) index. [R: ARBA 1990, pp. 518-9; Choice, Dec 89, p. 604; Notes, Dec 90, p. 390; RBB, Nov 1 1989, p. 602; WLB, Nov 89, p. 115]

176. Lee, William F. III. **People in Jazz**. Hialeah, FL: CPP Belwin, 1984. ISBN 0-89898-358-4. ML105.L38

A collection of brief biographies of more than 800 jazz pianists. It is divided into seven chronological areas, based on the artists birthdate (19th century; each decade from 1900 through the 1940s; and after 1950). The coverage includes all styles of jazz and blues and it includes an artist index.

177. Lyons, Len and Don Perlo. **Jazz Portraits: The Lives and Music of the Jazz Masters**. New York: William Morrow, 1989. 610p. LCCN 88-8929. ISBN 0-688-04946-X. ML394.L97

An alphabetically arranged collection of brief biographies of more than 200 jazz musicians. Though brief, the entries tend to be analytical, focusing on each artist's contributions to the art. It includes a glossary, a bibliography and a general index. [R: ARBA 1991, p. 532, Notes, Mar 91, pp. 791-2]

178. Lyons, Len. **The Great Jazz Pianists: Speaking of their Lives and Music**. New York: William Morrow, 1983. 321p. (reprinted by Da Capo, 1989) ISBN 0-306-80343-7. ML397G68

A collection of interviews with 27 famous jazz pianists. Each entry begins with a brief biography and includes a selective discography. It is indexed and includes a bibliography.

179.   Mapp, Edward. **Directory of Blacks in the Performing Arts**. 2d ed. Metuchen, NJ: Scarecrow, 1990. 612p. LCCN 78-2438. ISBN 0-8108-2222-9. PN1590.B53M3

A collection of personal data on Black performers in film, television, night clubs, stage, opera, ballet, jazz and classical concert. The focus is on (but not exclusive to) living artists. More than 800 artists are listed alphabetically. The entries simply list data and accomplishments (birth dates, address, honors, education, etc.).

180.   McGovern, Dennis and Deborah Grace. **Sing Out, Louise: 150 Stars of the Musical Theatre Remember 50 Years on Broadway**. New York: Schirmer Books, c1993. LCCN 92-33132. ISBN 0-02-871394-X. ML1711.8.N3M265

A collection of anecdotes collected from interviews of artists connected with the musical theater. It is divided into 16 broad topics (auditions, being on the road, understudies, etc.). The index lists both artists and show titles.

181.   McRae, Barry. **The Jazz Handbook**. Boston: G.K. Hall, 1989. 272p. LCCN 89-77757. ISBN 0-8161-9096-8. ML105.M455

Divided into seven chronological sections (pre-twenties, the twenties, the thirties, the forties, the fifties, the sixties, the seventies & eighties); each section begins with a brief commentary on the musical trends and developments of the period. This is followed by an alphabetically arranged selection of artist biographies. It is intended for the "jazz newcomer" and tends to be more critical than historical. Each entry will direct the reader to other artists who influenced, or were influenced by, the artist covered. Entries include selected discographies and bibliographies. Appendices include a glossary, a bibliography, a jazz record company directory, and a list of jazz magazine and festivals. It includes a general index. [R: ARBA 1991, pp. 532-3; Choice, Nov 90, p. 462; LJ, July 90, p. 88; RBB, Sept 1 1990, p. 87]

182.   Mellers, Wilfrid. **Angels of the Night: Popular Female Singers of our Time**. New York: Basil Blackwell, c1986. 275p. LCCN 85-18659. ISBN 0-631-14696-2. ML400.M44

A collection of biographies of women singers of popular music styles (folk, gospel, blues, rhythm and blues/soul, country and rock). More than 70 artists are featured. It includes a selected discography, a glossary and a general index.

183. Mulhern, Tom, ed. **Bass Heroes: Styles Stories and Secrets of Thirty Great Players**. San Francisco: GPI Publications/Miller Freeman, 1993. 208p. LCCN 92-45801. ISBN 0-87930-274-7. ML399.B39

A collection of articles and interviews of bass players (mostly electric) originally published in Guitar Player Magazine. Entries are divided by styles: Jazz (9 artists), Rock(12 artists), Funk & blues (4 artists), and Studio & pop (5 artists).

184. Nash, Alanna. **Behind Closed Doors: Talking with the Legends of Country Music**. New York: Alfred Knopf, 1988. 553p. LCCN 87-46321. ISBN 0-679-72102-9. ML385.N37

A collection of 27 interviews of country artists. Each entry begins with a brief biography. The interviews were conducted from 1975 through 1986 (though most tend to be more current).

185. **New Age Musicians**. GPI Collectors Edition. Cupertino, CA: GPI Publications, 1988. 66p. ML385.N53

A collection of profiles of 11 new age musicians. Each entry includes a photo and a selective discography. Some musical examples are included. All articles are reprinted from the GPI periodicals: Guitar Player Magazine, Keyboard Magazine, and Frets.

186. Nite, Norm N. **Rock On: The Illustrated Encyclopedia of Rock n' Roll, the Solid Gold Years.** Updated ed. New York: Harper & Row, 1982. LCCN 77-12247. ISBN 0-06-181642-6
——. **Rock On: The Illustrated Encyclopedia of Rock n' Roll, the Years of Change, 1964 to 1978.** Updated ed. New York: Harper & Row, 1984. LCCN 83-48371. ISBN 0-06-181643-4
——. **Rock On: The Illustrated Encyclopedia of Rock n' Roll, the Video Revolution, 1978 to Present**. New York: Harper & Row, 1985. LCCN 85-42723. ISBN 0-06-181644-2. ML105.N49

An alphabetically arranged biographical dictionary. The focus
is on artists with hit records during the indicated periods. All
commercial styles(soul, rockabilly, pop, etc.) of contemporary
popular music are represented. Entries are generally brief
with selected discographies of single recordings.

Volume one contains more than 1,000 popular musicians and
groups of the 1950s and early 1960s. The second volume lists
an additional 1,000+ popular musicians and groups with hit
records between 1964 and 1978. Volume three updates
through 1983. Each volume includes an index of song titles.
[R: ARBA 1976, pp. 491-2; BL, Mar 1 1975, p. 705; Choice,
May 75, pp. 372-4; WLB, Feb 75, p. 458 (volume 1); ARBA
1985, p. 441 (volume 2)]

187. Obrecht, Jas, ed. **Blues Guitar: The Men Who Made the
Music**. 2d ed. San Francisco: GPI Books, 1993. 278p. LCCN
93-6393. ISBN 0-87930-292-5. ML399.B53

A compilation of 31 interviews or biographical articles from
Guitar Player Magazine. It is divided into two sections
(Country Roots and Prime Movers). Entries include a selec-
tive discography and a name index is included.

188. Parish, James Robert and Michael R. Pitts. **Hollywood
Songsters**. New York: Garland, 1991. 826p. LCCN 90-
41110. ISBN 0-8240-3444-9. ML400.P295

A collection of biographies of 104 performers who have had
success as both film stars and singers. Each entry includes a
full biography, filmography and discography. [R: Notes, Sept
93, pp. 174-7]

189. Pleasants, Henry. **The Great American Popular Singers**.
New York: Simon & Schuster, 1974. 384p. LCCN 84-20251.
ISBN 0-671-54098-X; 0-671-54099-8 (pbk.). ML400.P647

A collection of biographies of 21 prominent popular music
vocalists. A broad range of styles are represented including
jazz, rhythm & blues and country. There is an index as well
as a glossary of terms. The entries do not include discographies.

190. Pringle, Colin G. **The Black Book**. Oxford, England: Solid

State Logic, 1990. 88p. ISBN 0-9516522-0-6.

A collection of profiles of 39 record producer/engineers. Each
entry lists album credits and includes photos. Developed as a
promotion for SSL audio mixing consoles (each artist is photo-
graphed next to one).

191. Rees, Dafydd and Luke Crampton, eds. **Rock Movers and
Shakers**. Santa Barbara, CA: ABC-Clio, 1991. 585p. LCCN
91-214326. ISBN 0-87436-661-5. ML385.R736

An alphabetically arranged listing of artists and ensembles of
the early rock era. Entries for groups first list the personnel
along with their instrument(s). Birthdates and birthplaces are
generally included in the beginning of each entry. Each entry
consists of a chronological list of significant career events;
divided by year (subdivided by month when necessary). [R:
ARBA 1992, p. 536; LJ, Nov 15 1991, p. 74; Notes, June 1993,
pp. 1509-10; RQ, Sum 92, pp. 578-9]

192. Richards, Tad and Melvin B. Shestack. **The New Country
Music Encyclopedia**. New York: Simon & Schuster, c1993.
270p. LCCN 93-17689. ISBN 0-671-78258-4. ML102.C7R5

A collection of brief biographies of about 200 country music
performers and groups. Each entry lists birth/death dates,
style (hillbilly, country pop, etc.), and best known songs. It
includes a selected discography of 101 country albums and an
index of names and titles.

193. **Rock Guitarists: From the Pages of Guitar Player
Magazine**. New York: Guitar Player Books, 1975. 171p.
LCCN 74-25847. ISBN 0-8256-9505-8
———. **Rock Guitarists: From the Pages of Guitar Player
Magazine, Volume II**. New York: Guitar Player Books,
1978. 214p. LCCN 77-087210. ISBN 0-8256-9506-6.
ML399.R62

A compilation of interviews and profiles of prominent rock
guitarists. The entries from volume one (70 total) were selected from issues of Guitar Player Magazine published from 1967
(their first year of publication) through 1974. Entries from
volume two (nearly 70 more entries) are from issues published

from 1975 through 1977. Both volumes include a few bass guitarists and each contains an index of guitarists names.

194.   Sallis, James. **The Guitar Players: One Instrument and Its Masters in American Music**. New York: William Morrow, 1982. 288p. LCCN 82-6403. ISBN 0-688-01375-9. ML399.S24

A collection of profiles of 12 guitarists. All are selected as seminal players; representing blues, jazz, country and popular music styles. It includes an index.

195.   Santelli, Robert. **The Big Book of the Blues: A Biographical Encyclopedia**. New York: Penguin Books, 1993. 448p. LCCN 93-4127. ISBN 0-140-15939-8. ML400.S227

A collection of brief (usually less then 1 page) biographies of about 600 blues and rhythm and blues artists. Entries include one to three recommended recordings - including reissues. [R: LJ, Jan 94, p. 110]

196.   Schaffner, Nicholas. **The British Invasion: From the First Wave to the New Wave**. New York: McGraw-Hill, 1983. 316p. LCCN 82-174. ISBN 0-07-055089-1. ML3534.S32

A biographical reference of British rock artists/ensembles, popular in the U.S. between 1964 and 1980. In part one, the author selects seven top performers (Beatles, Rolling Stones, Kinks, Who, Pink Floyd, T.Rex, and David Bowie) for more detailed (20 to 40 page) treatment. Part 2 contains 100 brief artist/ensemble profiles each including a discography. Part 3 is a year-by-year listing of recordings (singles) from the Billboard magazine Hot 100 charts of British artists. Part 4 is a chronology of British music events. [R: ARBA 1983, p. 448]

197.   Scott, Barry. **We Had Joy, We Had Fun: The "Lost" Recording Artists of the Seventies**. Winchester, MA: Faber and Faber, 1994. 237p. LCCN 93-46448. ISBN 0-571-19835-X. ML3534.S39

A collection of interviews with 21 pop music artists/groups from the 1970s. Each entry includes a discography of the artists' charted recordings listed with year and highest chart position.

198.   Shestack, Melvin. **The Country Music Encyclopedia**. New
       York: Crowell, 1974.   410p.   LCCN 74-9644.   ISBN 0-690-
       00442-7.   ML102.C7S5

       An alphabetical listing of over 200 country musicians (inclu-
       ding blue grass, country blues, etc.).   It also includes defini-
       tions of broad country terminology and styles.   Artists are
       selected for their commercial success.   It includes a selected
       discography and list of U.S. and Canadian country music radio
       stations.   [R: ARBA 1975, p. 513;   LJ, July 74, 1822;   WLB,
       Dec 74, p. 315]

199.   Simon, George T.   **The Big Bands**.   4th ed.   New York:
       Schirmer Books, 1981.   614p.   LCCN 81-51633.   ISBN 0-02-
       872420-8; 0-02-872430-5 (pbk.).   ML3518.S55

       A collection of profiles of 72 prominent big bands (listed by
       leader).   It begins with an overview of the history of the big
       band era.   This is followed by an alphabetically arranged col-
       lection of very brief profiles of more than 200 bands/band
       leaders.   It includes a selective discography and a list of big
       band theme songs.

200.   Small, Michael.   **Break It Down: The Inside Story of the
       New Leaders of Rap**.   New York: Citadel, 1992.   224p.
       LCCN 92-37445.   ISBN 0-8065-1361-1.   ML3531.S6

       A collection of brief interviews with 40 prominent rap artists.

201.   Smith, Joe and Michael Fink, ed.   **Off the Record: An Oral
       History of Popular Music**.   New York: Warner Books, 1989.
       429p.   LCCN 88-24068.   ISBN 0-446-51232-X.   ML3477.034

       A collection of brief quotations (average 2 pages) by more than
       200 jazz and popular music artists and record industry
       leaders.   Arrangement seems to be in a chronological order,
       though interview dates are not given.

202.   Smith, Steven C.   **Film Composers Guide**.   1st ed.   Beverly
       Hills, CA: Lone Eagles Publishing, 1990.   310p.   ISBN 0-
       943728-36-3

       An alphabetical arranged listing of living film composers, each with contact information, birthdate, and a chronological list of film credits. Each film listed includes a release date and distributor or production company. It includes an alphabetical listing of "notable film composers of the past", each with similar information. It also includes an index of film titles and a directory of agents and managers listed.

203.   Sonnier, Austin M. **A Guide to the Blues: History, Who's Who, Research Sources**. Westport, CT: Greenwood Press, 1994. LCCN 93-30773. ISBN 0-313-28724-4. ML3521.S58

A biographical dictionary of about 300 blues artists including birth/death dates, birthplaces, selected discographies and brief career profiles. It begins with a history of the blues (including some analysis) from its African roots to its present popular music influences. It also includes a selected filmography, a selected bibliography and a selected discography. The history and biography sections are indexed with cross references.

204.   Southern, Eileen. **Biographical Dictionary of Afro-American and African Musicians**. Westport, CT: Greenwood Press, 1982. 496p. LCCN 81-2586. ISBN 0-313-21339-9. ML105.S67

A biographical dictionary of more than 1,500 musicians of African descent from the 17th to the 20th century. The focus is on Americans and it encompasses all musical styles. Three appendices cross-reference the entries by (1) period of birth, (2) place of birth and (3) musical occupations. It contains a bibliography and general name index. [R: ARBA 1983, p. 449; LJ, Jan 1 1982, pp. 85-6]

205.   Spagnardi, Ron. **The Great Jazz Drummers**. edited by William F. Miller. Cedar Grove, NJ: Modern Drummer Publications, 1992. 128p. ISBN 0-7935-1526-2

A collection of brief profiles of 62 prominent jazz drummers from the 1920s to the present. Each is less than one page in length and is accompanied by a photograph of the artist. It includes a sound sheet of recorded examples of 16 of the drummers profiled.

206.   Stambler, Irwin and Grelun Landon. **The Encyclopedia of**

Folk, Country & Western Music. 2d ed. New York: St. Martin's Press, 1983. 902p. LCCN 82-5702. ISBN 0-312-24818-0. ML102.F66S7

A biographical dictionary of more than 600 artists and groups from the folk and country music fields (including bluegrass, folk rock, rockabilly, etc.). Entries are alphabetical and include birth dates and places, and a brief career profile. Although the commentaries include some information on recordings, discographies are not included. [R: ARBA 1984, p. 451; BL, Jan 1 1983, p. 595; LJ, Jan 1 1983, p. 43; WLB, Mar 83, p. 607]

207.   Stambler, Irwin. **Encyclopedia of Pop, Rock and Soul**. rev. ed. New York: St. Martin's Press, 1989. 887p. LCCN 88-29860. ISBN 0-312-02573-4. ML102.P66S8

A biographical dictionary of rock era recording artists. Each entry begins with basic data such as group personnel; birth-dates; and birth places. The biographies average from one to two pages, more important artists are longer. It includes appendices of Grammy Awards (1958-1988), Academy Awards (music 1958-1988), and RIAA Gold Record Awards (1958-1988). [R: ARBA 1990, p. 549; LJ, Feb 15 1989, p. 156; RBB, June 15 1989, pp. 1802-3]

208.   Stone, Terri, ed. **Music Producers: Conversations with Today's Top Record Makers**. Emeryville, CA: Mixbooks, 1992. 117p. LCCN 92-070769. ISBN 0-7935-1418-5

A collection of interviews with 25 successful record producers. Subjects range from rap producer KRS-One to journeyman George Martin. Entries are four or five pages long and begin with a brief career biography. All interviews were previously published in Mix magazine.

209.   Summerfield, Maurice J. **The Jazz Guitar: Its Evolution and its Players**. Gateshead, Eng.: Ashley Mark, 1978. 238p. ISBN 0-9506224-0-0. ML399.S9

A biographical dictionary of 116 jazz guitarists. Each entry includes a very brief biography, a selected discography, and a bibliography. It also includes brief descriptive articles about selected jazz guitars.

210. Sumrall, Harry. **Pioneers of Rock and Roll: 100 Artists Who Changed the Face of Rock**. Billboard Hit Makers Series. New York: Billboard Books/Watson-Guptill, 1994. 307p. LCCN 93-44847. ISBN 0-8230-7628-8. ML102.R6S85

An alphabetical listing of 100 artists/groups that had the most significant impact on rock music. Rock music is defined narrowly, excluding blues, rhythm and blues, country, and pop oriented artists. Impact is not measured by record sales but by influence and innovation. Entries are both historical and critical, and each includes a selected discography. The index lists artists, song titles, and album titles.

211. Tee, Ralph. **Soul Music Who's Who.** Rocklin, CA: Prima Pub., 1992. 320p. LCCN 92-23109. ISBN 0-55958-226-6. ML102.S65T43

An alphabetical listing of the performers, songwriters and producers of American soul music, from the 1960s to the present. Entries include brief professional histories with cross-references indicated in bold type.

212. Thomson, Liz, ed. **New Women in Rock**. New York: Delilah/Putnam, 1982. 96p. LCCN 82-10027. ISBN 0-399-41003-1. ML82.N5

A collection of brief biographies of over 70 female rock artists. The careers of most of the artists listed centered around the late 1970s. Focus is on rock and punk artists, practically eliminating R & B performers. A discography is included for each artist listed.

213. Tobler, John and Stuart Grundy. **The Record Producers**. New York: St. Martin's Press, 1983. 248p. LCCN 82-16855. ISBN 0-312-66594-6. ML3790.T62

A collection of biographies of thirteen producers of contemporary popular records. Six are American; seven are British. Each entry includes a discography. The index includes artists, groups, song titles and LP titles.

214. Tobler, John. **The Guitar Greats**. New York: St. Martin's Press, 1983. 192p. LCCN 83-15926. ISBN 0-312-35319-7. ML399.T64

A collection of 14 biographies of rock guitarists. Each entry includes a discography. An index of artist names is included. [R: ARBA 1985, p. 423; LJ, Feb 1 1984, p. 182]

215.   Tobler, John. **Guitar Heroes**. New York: St. Martin's Press, 1978. 88p. LCCN 78-438. ISBN 0-312-35320-0. ML399.T65

Very brief profiles of 32 rock (and a few blues) guitar players. It is divided into three sections: pioneers, superstars, and specialists. Each entry includes a selective album discography.

216.   Tobler, John. **MTV Music Television, Who's Who in Rock Video.** 1st Quill ed. New York: Quill, 1984. 190p. LCCN 84-60325 ISBN 0-6880-4042-X ML105.M75

A collection of brief portraits of rock artists and groups that have been influential in music video. The articles are brief, are broadly biographical, and have little if any focus or insight into the processes of video production or the effects of music videos on the artist's careers. Of note, this book contains two indexes of video directors, one by director's names, the other by recording artist.

217.   Tobler, John. **Who's Who in Rock & Roll**. New York: Crescent Books, 1991. 350p. ISBN 0-517-05687-9. ML156.4.J3T73

Alphabetically arranged brief biographies of 500 rock bands and performers. The entries for bands include personnel and each entry includes a selected discography. It includes photos of most artists listed.

218.   Tosches, Nick. **Unsung Heroes of Rock 'n' Roll**. New York: Harmony, 1991. 276p. LCCN 90-47515. ISBN 0-517-58052-7. ML394.T67

A collection of 25 portraits of R & B and rockabilly artists that, between 1945 and 1955, had a direct influence on the development of rock music. It includes discographies for each artist covered as well as a list of reissues on compact disc. It also includes an index of names.

219.   Traum, Artie and Arti Funaru. **The Legends of Rock**

Guitar. New York: Oak Publications, 1986. 71p. ISBN 0-8256-0309-9. ML399.T75

Collected profiles of 12 prominent rock guitarists. The entries are more analytical than biographical. The focus is on the many musical examples (mostly short transcriptions) included for each artist.

220. Unterbrink, Mary. **Jazz Women at the Keyboard**. Jefferson, NC: McFarland, 1983. 184p. LCCN 83-756. ISBN 0-89950-074-9. ML397.U57

A collection of biographical sketches of more than 50 female jazz musicians. Most entries are brief except for a special focus on Mary Lou Williams and Lil Hardin Armstrong. Entries are mostly arranged by geographic area and it includes a name indexed.

221. Vaughan, Andrew. **Who's Who in New Country Music**. New York: St. Martin's Press, c1989. 128p. LCCN 89-27126. ISBN 0-312-03953-0. ML105 .V25

A collection of brief sketches of American country music artists popular in the 1980s. Most entries include an illustration.

222. Walker, Leo. **The Big Band Almanac**. Pasadena, CA: Ward Richie Press, 1978. Reprinted by Da Capo, 1989. 466p. LCCN 88-33463. ISBN 0-306-80345-3. ML102.B5

An alphabetical listing of about 250 big band leaders (from the 1920s through the 1950s). Each entry includes a career profile along with a list of sidemen, vocalists, the theme song, and record company affiliations. All personnel are listed in an index. [R: ARBA 1980, p. 444]

223. Warner, Jay. **Billboard Book of American Singing Groups: A History, 1940-1990**. New York: Billboard/Watson-Guptill, 1992. LCCN 92-18328. ISBN 0-8230-8264-4. ML106.U3W2

A guide to more than 350 pop music vocal groups (including jazz, R&B, Doo Wop, and soul styles). Groups are listed alphabetically under the decade they first became popular (50s through 80s) Each entry includes a brief biography (including all personnel and changes to personnel) and a comprehensive discography of single releases. [R: ARBA 1994, p. 556]

224.   Weinberg, Max. **The Big Beat: Conversations with Rock's Great Drummers**. New York: Watson-Guptill, 1991. LCCN 91-3981. ISBN 0-8230-7571-0. ML3534.W44

A collection of interviews with 17 prominent contemporary rock drummers.

225.   Welding, Pete and Toby Byron, eds. **Bluesland: Portraits of Twelve Major American Blues Masters**.   New York: Dutton, 1991. 253 p. LCCN 91-14653. ISBN 0-525-93375-1. ML400.B595

A collection of biographies of twelve famous blues artists. It is richly illustrated but lacks both discography and indexing.

226.   White, Mark.   **'You Must Remember This...': Popular Songwriters 1900-1980**. New York: Scribner's, 1985. 304p. LCCN 85-1974. ISBN 0-684-18433-8. ML390.W378

An alphabetical arranged collection of biographies of more than 130 popular songwriters. Each entry include a selective list of songs. It contains four indexes: (1) song titles, (2) performers, (3) composers and lyricists, and (4) musical shows and films. [R: ARBA 1986, p. 498; Choice, Sept 85, p. 90]

227.   **Who's Who in Entertainment, 1992-1993**.   2d rev. ed. Wilmette, IL: Marquis Who's Who, 1992. 768p. ISBN 0-8379-1851-0. PN1583.W47

An alphabetically arranged collection of nearly 17,000 brief biographical sketches of individuals in the entertainment industry. Less than a third of the entries are high-profile musicians and actors. The remainder include broadcast executives, music educators, composers, screenwriters, cinematographers, dancers, film directors and producers, engineers, video specialists, radio and television personalities, comedians, choreographers, critics, dance and recording studio owners, clowns, cartoonists, costume designers and puppeteers.

Entries include birthdates, birthplaces, career accomplishments, and addresses.

228.   York, William. **Who's Who in Rock Music**. Revised ed.
       New York: Scribner's, 1982.   413p.   ISBN 0-684-17342-5.
       ML102.R6Y7

       A collection of very brief profiles of more than 12,000 artists
       and groups. It is arranged alphabetically and is very useful
       for cross-referencing artists' names with the groups they are
       affiliated with (and vice-versa).   Coverage is strongest for
       artists that recorded after 1960.   [R: ARBA 1983, p. 450;
       Choice, Sept 82, p. 62; LJ, Apr 1 1982, p 720; WLB, Sept 82,
       p. 78]

Dictionaries of Terms

229. Anderton, Craig. **The Electronic Musicians Dictionary**. New York: Amsco Publications, 1988. 119p. LCCN 88-176371. ISBN 0-8256-1125-3. ML102.E4A5

An alphabetically arranged collection of more than 1,000 music synthesis and record engineering terms defined. Even though the definitions were written for a beginner's comprehension, the scope of this book is broad enough to include more subtle professional terminology.

230. Burke, David. **Street Talk 2: Slang Used by Teens, Rappers, Surfers & Popular American Television Shows**. Los Angeles: Optima Books, c1992. 286p. LCCN 92-81410. ISBN 1-879440-06-7. PE2846.B89

Part of an entertaining series on American slang. This volume focuses upon the language of contemporary teen culture.

231. Cary, Tristram. **Dictionary of Musical Technology**. Westport, CT: Greenwood Press, 1992. 576p. LCCN 92-14583. ISBN 0-313-28694-9. ML102.E4C37

A collection of more than 800 definitions of terms associated with electronic instruments, music synthesis, and computer music. [R: Choice, Mar 1993, p. 1106; Notes, Mar 1994, pp. 1021-23]

232. Dobson, Richard. **Dictionary of Electronic and Computer Music Technology: Instruments, Terms, Techniques**.

New York: Oxford, 1992. 224p. LCCN 92-165311. ISBN 0-19-311344-9. ML102.E4D6

An electronic music dictionary focused on broad principles and techniques. Along with many brief descriptions, the author also includes longer comprehensive subject entries (acoustics, computer, etc.) that are referred to throughout the text. There are three indexes: product names, personal names, and a general index of terms. [R: Notes, Mar 1994, pp. 1021-23]

233.   Fink, Robert and Robert Ricci. **The Language of Twentieth Century Music: A Dictionary of Terms**. New York: Schirmer Books, 1975. 175p. LCCN 74-13308. ISBN 0-02-870600-5. ML100.F55

An alphabetically arranged collection of important terms found in avant-garde music, and popular music forms. It includes terminology related to computer music, electronic music synthesis and production, and film music. An appendix contains all listed terms divided by subject or topic. [R: ARBA 1976, p. 477; Choice, Jan 1976, p. 14; LJ, Oct 1 1975, p. 1810]

234.   Gold, Robert S. **Jazz Talk: A Dictionary of the Colorful Language that has Emerged from America's Own Music**. Indianapolis: Bobbs-Merrill, 1975. Reprinted by Da Capo, 1982. LCCN 74-17642. ISBN 0-306-76155-6. ML102.J3G7

An alphabetical arrangement of more than 1,000 terms and expressions associated with jazz. Each term is defined then displayed in context through dated quotes. All sources are listed in a bibliography. (First edition: A jazz lexicon. New York: Alfred A. Knopf, 1964.) [R: ARBA 1976, p. 490; Notes, Dec 75, p. 302; WLB, Nov 75, p. 265]

235.   Lee, Bill. **Bill Lee's Jazz Dictionary**. New York: Shattinger International Music Corp., 1979. 64p. ISBN 0-8494-0159-3. ML102.J3L43

A collection of very brief definitions of more than 2,500 terms related to jazz. It includes styles and idioms, instruments and instrumentation, as well as musicians' slang. Also included are terms from music synthesis, audio engineering and computers. A list of Down Beat Award winners, from 1937 to 1978 is also included.

236. Livingston, Robert Allen. **Music Industry Business and Law Reference Book**. Cardiff by the Sea, CA: GLGLC Music, 1988. 2v. Volume 1: ISBN 0-932303-13-7; 0-932303-15-3(pap). Volume 2: ISBN 0-932303-14-5; 0-932303-16-1 (pbk.). KF4291.A68L58

Each volume contains alphabetically arranged definitions of music industry terms. The terms are within the areas of business, taxes, law, marketing and advertising. It is not clear what criteria is used to decide which volume an entry belongs in, although entries in volume two tend to be longer - some article length. There is an accumulative index of all terms covered as well as secondary terms from the text.

237. Progris, Jim. **Language of Commercial Music**. New York: Charles Hansen, [?]. 32p. ML102.M85P8

Alphabetically arranged list of about 400 terms with brief definitions. Coverage "includes publishing, copyright, promotion, marketing, radio, recording and entertainment industry terms." (foreword)

238. Rachlin, Harvey. **The Encyclopedia of the Music Business**. New York: Harper & Row, 1981. 524p. LCCN 81-47235. ISBN 0-06-014914-2. ML102.M85R3

An alphabetical listing of over 450 definitions of terms and concepts of the music industry. Areas included are copyright and contracts; music recording and publishing industries; recording and production (technical terms); unions and trade associations; and radio. Appendices include: (1) acronyms and abbreviations; (2) copyright forms; (3) Academy Awards (music); (4) Grammy Awards; (5) Tony Awards; and (6) gold record awards (all awards through 1980). [R: ARBA 1982, pp. 507-8; BL, Sept 1 1981, p. 9]

239. Tomlyn, Bo and Steve Leonard. **Electronic Music Dictionary: A Glossary of the Specialized Terms Relating to the Music and Sound Technology of Today**. Milwaukee: Hal Leonard Books, 1988. 77p. LCCN 88-614. ISBN 0-88188-904-0. ML102.E4T65

More than 300 definitions of terms relating to synthesizers, amplification, MIDI, and computers in music-making.

240.   Wadhams, Wayne. **Dictionary of Music Production and Engineering Terminology**. New York: Schirmer Books, 1988. LCCN 87-30998. ISBN 0-02-872691-X. ML102.M85W3

An alphabetical listing of music engineering and music business terminology. It includes the areas of music publishing, synthesis, and advertising. Both formal terms and jargon are included. It is broad in scope and illustrated. It also includes a list of standard units and measures, and a bibliography. [R: ARBA 1989, p. 471; RQ, Sum 88, p. 570]

241.   White, Glenn D. **The Audio Dictionary**. Seattle: University of Washington Press, 1987. 291p. LCCN 87-15939. ISBN 0-295-96527-4. TK7881.4.W48

An alphabetically arranged collection of definitions of terminology and concepts of sound recording, sound reinforcement and musical acoustics. It covers the areas of electro-acoustics, audio electronics, digital audio, and psycho-acoustics. The seven appendices are articles discussing selected topics in greater detail. It includes a bibliography. [R: RBB, Feb 1 1992, p. 1052]

Directories

242. **Billboard Nashville 615/Country Music Sourcebook 1994.** Annual. New York: BPI Communications, 1994. 106p. ISBN 0-8230-8075-7

A national directory of country music record labels, publishers, artists, managers/agents, concert promoters, venues, record producers, associations and radio stations. Entries include addresses, phone/fax numbers and contact names. It also includes non-country listings from the Nashville area (the Nashville 615 section).

243. **Billboard 1994 International Buyer's Guide.** Annual. 35th ed. New York: BPI Communications, 1994. 278p. ISBN 0-8239-8064-1. ML18.B5

An up-to-date directory for the recording industry. U.S. entries are divided by the headings: record labels; video companies; music publishers; sheet music suppliers; wholesalers and distributors; industry services and suppliers; and manufacturing plants and equipment. Entries are listed alphabetically under appropriate headings and include addresses, telephone and fax numbers, and company officers. Some headings are subdivided by state. European and Asian listings are divided by country and further subdivided by similar headings.

244. **Billboard's 1995 International Talent and Touring Directory.** Annual. New York: BPI Communications, 1991.

234p. ISBN 0-8230-8079-X

A directory for the concert promotion field. The first section is
an alphabetical listing of U.S. and International performing
artists with their current record label, booking agent, personal
managers, public relations and business management firms.
This is followed by an alphabetical list of agents/managers
with addresses, telephone numbers and key personnel. These
key sections are followed by listings for U.S. tour venues and
services, insurance companies, and facility equipment manufacturers. These are followed by similar International listings.

245.   Bond, Sherry.   **Songwriter's & Musician's Guide to
        Nashville**. Cincinnati: Writer's Digest Books, 1991. 176p.
        LCCN 91-23199. ISBN 0-89879-457-9. ML3790.S66

        A directory of Nashville music services that includes manag-
        ers, agents, producers, publishers, legal services, record manu-
        facturers, as well as many music related services (e.g. public
        relations, photographers, etc.). It also includes a collection of
        articles and interviews designed to introduce the songwriter to
        the Nashville music scene.

246.   Byrczak, Jan A. **Jazz in the U.S.A. Directory**. New York:
        Jazz World Database, 1993.

        A listing of contacts and addresses all associated with jazz
        music.   It includes artists/bands, venues, education, record
        labels/distributors/stores, magazines/press contacts, and radio
        contacts.

247.   Dorf, Michael Ethan and Robert Appel, eds. **Gigging: The
        Musician's Underground Touring Directory**. Cincinnati:
        Writer's Digest Books, 1989. LCCN 89-16658. ISBN 0-89879-
        356-4. ML17.G53

        A directory designed for promoting the "alternate rock" band.
        It lists appropriate venues (clubs), record stores, radio sta-
        tions, and press contacts. Entries are listed by geographic
        area. [R: ARBA 1991, p. 526]

248.   Fuchs, Michael, ed. **Recording Industry Sourcebook,
        1992**. Annual. Los Angeles, CA: Ascona Communications,

c1992. 597p. LCCN 92-641797. ISSN: 1060-9075. ML18.R4

A broad industry directory covering all areas of record, video, and concert production. Entries include addresses; telephone numbers; fax numbers; and executives and/or contacts. Entries are divided by subjects including: record labels and distributors; managers and agents; record producers and engineers; promotion and marketing; recording studios; equipment sales and rentals; and numerous related manufacturing and service businesses and professionals. Also included are listings for associations and schools that offer programs in audio recording. This directory is also available in electronic form. (See appendix C)

249. Laufenberg, Cindy, ed. **1994 Songwriters Market: Where and How to Market Your Songs**. Cincinnati: Writer's Digest Books, 1993. 522p. ISBN 0-89879-610-5. ISSN 0161-5971. MT67.S657

A directory of music publishers, record companies, record producers, managers and booking agents, advertising and commercial music firms, play producers and publishers, and fine arts organizations. It includes lists of songwriter's organizations, workshops, contests, and awards. Each annual edition is extensively revised and updated and includes a selection of articles pertaining to different aspects of songwriting. The latest edition includes more than 2,500 entries and features a category index that arranges contacts into 18 musical types. [R: Choice, Mar 1994, p. 1104]

250. Kruglinski, Susan, Jim Staley and David Weinstein. **Einstein's Guide to the Musical Universe**. New York: Roulette Intermedium, Inc., c1993.

A business directory for "non-mainstream music" including experimental, 20th century classical, avant jazz, and fringe indie rock. It lists clubs, concert halls, newspapers and magazines, radio stations, journalists, record stores, arts councils and support organizations, music schools, collections, and distributors. It includes an alphabetical index of entries.

251. Levine, Michael. **The Music Address Book**. New York: Harper & Row, 1989. LCCN 89-45102. ISBN 0-06-096383-2. ML17.L4 1989

A selective list of addresses for recording artists, record producers, record companies, songwriters, disc jockeys, music
journalists and music video directors. [R: ARBA 1991, p. 527]

252. **Musicians Guide to Touring and Promotion**. New York:
      BPI Communications, 1994. 153p.

A special annual publication of Musician Magazine aimed at
promotion of the new independent artist or group. It contains
a city by city guide to clubs, radio stations, press and record
stores. It also contains listings of record labels and their A&R
staffs, music publishers, new artist showcases, legal services,
and recording studios.

253. **Pollstar Concert Venue Directory, Winter 1994-1995**.
      Fresno, CA: Promoters On-Line Listings, 1994. 160p.

An international directory of concert venues. It is divided
geographically: by U.S. state, Canadian province, then all
remaining countries. Each entry includes the name of the
facility, address, phone/fax numbers, contacts, capacity and
rent. It includes a listing by company/facility name; and a
listing by personnel names.

254. Robinson, Doris. **Music and Dance Periodicals: An
      International Directory and Guide Book**. Voorheesville,
      NY: The Peri Press, 1989. 382p. LCCN 89-151380. ISBN 0-
      9617844-4-X. ML128.P24R58

Entries are listed alphabetically within the subject areas: reference; musicology & ethnomusicology; music industry,
musical instruments; regional; education; classical; religious &
choral; opera - theater - show music; band; composers & songwriters; computer & electronic; popular; jazz & blues; folk
music; sound; and miscellaneous. Entries are similar to
Urlich's and include some descriptive annotations.

255. Schreiber, Norman. **The Ultimate Guide to Independent
      Record Labels and Artists: An A-to-Z Guide to the Indie
      Music Scene**. New York: Pharos Books, 1992. 261p. LCCN
      92-11128. ISBN 0-88687-687-7. ML18.S38

An alphabetical list of independent record companies. Each

entry includes an address, phone number, contact person(s), type of music recorded, a list of artists recorded, and a brief history of the recording company. It includes an index of recording artists.

General Discographies

256. Albert, George and Frank Hoffmann, comps. **The Cash Box Black Contemporary Singles Charts, 1960-1984**. Metuchen, NJ: Scarecrow, 1986. 704p. LCCN 85-22078. ISBN 0-8108-1853-1. ML156.4.P6A42

An index to all recordings that appeared on the Cash Box (magazine) Black Contemporary Singles Charts from 1960 to 1984. (The chart had several different names during this time, such as: "Hot 100 R&B Chart".) The main body is an alphabetical list of artists and ensembles followed by an alphabetical list of their singles. Each entry includes the song title; record company and catalog number; the date that the record first appeared on the chart; the total weeks charted; and the record's chart position for each week that it charted. It includes an index linking songs titles to the artist(s) that recorded them. [R: ARBA, 1987 p. 492; LJ, June 1, 1986, p. 155; RBB Aug 86, p. 1672]

257. Bartlette, Reginald J. **Off the Record: Motown by Master Number, 1959-1989**. v.1: Singles. Ann Arbor, MI: Popular Culture, 1991. 508p. ISBN 1-56075-003-0. ML 156.4 R6B37

A listing of all Motown single releases, through 1989, by master number. Entries include song title, artist(s), duration, catalog number and date. It includes a performer index and a title index. [R: Choice, Apr 92, p. 1203]

258. Bianco, David. **Heat Wave: The Motown Fact Book**. Ann Arbor, MI: Popular Culture, 1988. 524p. LCCN 86-60558.

ISBN 1-56075-011-1. ML156.4.S6B5

The discography Motown Records releases.   Entries are
divided by label name and recording type (single, LP, etc.).
They are then listed alphabetically by artist and include song
title, matrix number, and session date.   There is an
artist/group index, a song/record title index, a date index, and
a record number index for both U.S. and U.K. listings. The
book also includes biographies of selected Motown artists and
a Motown chronology. [R: ARBA 1989, pp. 492-3; WLB, Oct
88, pp. 108-9]

259.   Blackstone, Orin. **Index to Jazz: Jazz Recordings 1917-
       1944**. Fairfax, VA:[private printing], 1945-48. 4 v. Reprinted
       by Greenwood Press, 1978. 1 v. 444p. LCCN 77-27076. ISBN
       0-313-20178-1. ML156.4.J3B6

Intended for the record collector and compiled from Record
Changer (a magazine). It is arranged alphabetically by artist
followed by a chronological list of recordings. Entries include
personnel, catalog number, and song titles. Cross-references
are included for many artists, indicating recordings they
appeared on as sidemen or recordings released under a group
name. [R: ARBA 1980, p. 440; RSR, July 1978, p. 7]

260.   Blair, John, comp. **The Illustrated Discography of Hot
       Rod Music 1961-1965**. Ann Arbor, MI: Popular Culture, Ink,
       1990. 167p. LCCN 89-92312. ISBN 0-56075-002-2.
       ——. **The Illustrated Discography of Surf Music, 1961-
       1965**. 2d ed. Ann Arbor, MI: Pierian Press, 1985. 166p. (Rock
       & Roll Reference Series, Vol. 15) LCCN 84-61227. ISBN 0-
       87650-174-9. ML156.4.R6B6

The first title is a listing of recordings, from the early 1960s,
that were about automobiles or automobile racing. The second
title is a discography of recordings with surfing as the subject
or (in the case of instrumental groups) with a distinctive surf
sound (a typical instrumentation described in the introduction). The format of both are the same.
  They are each divided into two sections: singles and albums,
with each section arranged alphabetically by artist. Entries
include dates, labels and catalog numbers, and most include a
brief biographical sketch. Singles entries list B-sides, while
album entries list all song title selections. Both include three
indexes: personal and group names; record labels and

numbers; and song and album titles. [R: ARBA 1991, pp. 534-5; Choice, Sept 90, p. 70; WLB, June 90, p. 148 (Surf Music): ARBA 1986, p. 501; RBB, July 85, p. 1524 (Hot Rod Music)]

261. Bronson, Fred. **Billboard's Hottest Hot 100 Lists**. New York: Watson-Guptill, 1991. LCCN 91-26029. ISBN 0-8230-7570-2. ML156.4.P6B77

A collection of "top" lists extracted from Billboard singles charts. Lists include top songs lists for: prominent artists, writers and producers; record labels; specific years; configurations (by male solo artist, by husband and wife, etc.); and subjects (songs about places, animals, etc.). The author includes a compilation of the top 3,000 hits, and includes an index of song titles.

262. Bruyninckx, Walter, comp. **60 Years of Recorded Jazz, 1917-1977**. Mechelen, Belgium: Walter Bruyninckx, 1978-80. (Updates *50 Years of Recorded Jazz, 1917-1967*, 1967-75.) ML156.4.J3B88

Published as loose pages over a three year period, this is probably the most complete general jazz discography available. It is over 11,000 pages long and covers, beyond jazz, into gospel and blues. Artists are listed alphabetically followed by a chronological list of recordings with personnel, record label and catalog number. Some artists have brief biographies. Because it was published over a long period of time many citations date beyond 1977 - as far as 1981. There is an index of sidemen. An update, of about 1,500 additional loose pages, was published in 1985. This, unfortunately, only updates from A to G.

263. Bruyninckx, Walter, comp. **Modern Big Band Discography [Jazz: Modern Jazz, Modern Big Band]**. Mechelen, Belgium: Walter Bruyninckx; Redwood, NY: Cadence Magazine, 1984-89. 2 v. LCCN 86-165245. ML156.4.B5B8

An update of the authors monumental work limited to modern big band jazz such as Don Ellis and Gil Evans. It includes an artist index.

264. Bruyninckx, Walter, comp. **Modern Discography [Jazz: Modern Jazz, Bebop, Hard Bop, West Coast]**. Mechelen, Belgium: Walter Bruyninckx; Redwood, NY: Cadence

Magazine, 1984-88. 6 v. LCCN 86-165225. ML156.4.J3B82

Another update of the authors initial discography limited to bop players. The session dates covered range from 1917 to 1982-85 (depending on the volume). It can be argued that some recordings listed here should be listed in the Progressive Jazz series. It includes an artist index.

265. Bruyninckx, Walter, comp. **Progressive Discography [Progressive Jazz: Free, Third Stream, Fusion]**. Mechelen, Belgium: Walter Bruyninckx; Redwood, NY: Cadence Magazine, 1984-89. 5 v. LCCN 86-165241. ML156.4.J3B83

One of the six update of the authors monumental work. This title is limited to free, third stream, fusion and avant-garde music. Entries range from 1917 to 1982-85 (depending on the volume). Volume five contains an artist index and an addenda of overlooked items and new listings.

266. Bruyninckx, Walter, comp. **Swing Discography [Swing, 1920-1985: Swing-Dance Bands & Combos]**. Mechelen, Belgium: Walter Bruyninckx; Redwood, NY: Cadence Magazine, 1986-91. 12 v. LCCN 86-165282. ML156.4.J3B87

An extensive discography of pre-bop style jazz. It covers both dance bands and small groups, focused on mainstream swing. This is the largest of the six focused discographies by Bruyninckx. It includes an artist index.

267. Bruyninckx, Walter, comp. **Traditional Discography [Jazz: Traditional Jazz, 1897-1985: Origins, New Orleans, Dixieland, Chicago Styles]**. Mechelen, Belgium: Walter Bruyninckx; Redwood, NY: Cadence Magazine, 1987-91. 5 v. ML156.4.J3B822

A comprehensive discography of pre-swing style jazz, including ragtime and some pre-jazz styles. Volume five contains an artist index.

268. Bruyninckx, Walter, comp. **Vocalists Discography [Jazz: The Vocalists, 1917-1986: Singers & Crooners]**. Mechelen, Belgium: Walter Bruyninckx; Redwood, NY: Cadence Magazine, 1988-91. 4 v. ML156.4.J3B796

Of all of Bruyninckx's discographies, this takes the broadest view of what jazz is and includes many blues, rhythm and blues, soul and pop vocalists (though many of these are selective). Volume four contains an artist index.

269.   **Catalog of the William Ransom Hogan Jazz Archive: The Collection of Seventy-eight RPM Phonograph Recordings**. Boston: G.K. Hall & Co., 1984. 2v. ISBN 0-8161-0434.

A discography 78 rpm jazz recordings held at the Howard Tilton Memorial Library at Tulane University. It is a photo reproduction of the card catalog of this important recorded jazz archive. Entries are included for song titles (both A and B sides), main artist, as well as many sidemen.

270.   **Christian Music Directories: Recorded Music 1993**. San Jose, CA: Resource Publications, 1993.

A comprehensive discography of Christian music including Gospel and instrumental recordings. It is arranged in three sections: a song index (listing artists with album titles, record labels and catalog numbers); an artist index (listing album titles, all album selections, record labels and catalog numbers); and an album title index (listing artists,, record labels and catalog numbers). It also includes an index of accompaniment tracks (listed by title), an index of music videos (listed by artist), and a directory of record labels and video publishers.

271.   Clee, Ken.   **The Directory of American 45 R.P.M. Records**. Philadelphia: Stak-O-Wax, 1989. 4v.

Printed loose leafed and updated periodically, this is a guide to all 45 rpm records released in the U.S. Volume one lists all recordings by the top 12 labels. Under each label, records are arranged by matrix number listing the artist, and both the A and B-side song titles. Volumes two lists about 400 smaller labels and their recordings while volume four lists the remaining obscure labels. Volume three is a compilation of about 400 major artists and their 45s, listing matrix numbers and A and B song titles.

272.   Cuscuna, Michael and Michel Ruppli, comps. **The Blue Note**

Label: A Discography. New York: Greenwood Press, 1988. 510p. (Discographies, no. 29; ISSN 0192-334X) LCCN 88-162. ISBN 0-313-22018-2. ML156.4.J3C87

A "discographical listing of all recordings made or issued on the Blue Note label" (preface). Within each of the first five parts of this book, recordings are arranged chronologically and list: the artist; the album title (when appropriate); the sidemen and the instruments they played (when information is available); the session date; and song titles with master and issue numbers. Parts six through nine index the recordings by issue numbers and part ten is an artist index (includes sidemen). [R: ARBA 1989, p. 491; Choice, Mar 89, pp. 1172, 1174]

273.   Delaunay, Charles. **New Hot Discography**. New York: Criterion Music Corp., 1948. 608p. ISBN 0-910468-04-4. ML156.4.J3D42

A classic discography of recorded jazz. It is divided into two major parts: pioneers of jazz; and post-1930 jazz. The first part is subdivided into: (1) New Orleans; (2) great blues singers; (3) first large bands; (4) other early bands and musicians; (5) New Orleans revival; (6) early Dixieland jazz; (7) Chicago; and (8) New York. The second part covers from 1930 to about 1947 and is arranged alphabetically by artist. Entries include recording dates, matrix and catalog numbers, personnel and song titles. All artist and ensemble names are included in an index.

274.   Dixon, Robert M.W. and John Godrich, comps. **Blues & Gospel Records: 1902-1943**. 3rd revised ed. Essex, Eng.: Storyville, 1982. 900p. ISBN 0-902391-03-8. ML156.4.B6D6

Arranged alphabetically by artist, the authors attempted to list virtually all recorded Black folk music, or "race records", from the period. Entries include song titles, dates, matrix and catalog numbers, and personnel or description of the recording.

275.   Downey, Pat. **The Golden Age of Top 40 Music (1955-1973) on Compact Disc**. Boulder, CO: Pat Downey Enterprises, 1992. 453p. LCCN 92-90455. ISBN 0-9633718-0-0. ML156.4.P6D69

Designed to assist in locating specific recordings that were originally issued between 1955 and 1973 and have since been reissued on compact disc. It is an alphabetical list of all artists and groups that had recordings listed in the top 40 positions of Cash Box singles charts. Under each artist/group is listed all of their top 40 titles with year of release and peak chart position. Those titles that have been reissued on audio CDs are indicated with the CD title, label, catalog number, timing and an indication whether the track is stereo, mono or electronic (originally monophonic but later electronically processed to appear stereo). The index lists all of the song titles covered and indicates which are reissued. [R: ARBA 1994, p. 557]

276.   Duxbury, Jannell R. **Rockin' the Classics and Classicizin' the Rock: A Selectively Annotated Discography**. Westport, CT: Greenwood Press, 1985. 188p. LCCN 84-22419. ISBN 0-313-24605-X
——. **Rockin' the Classics and Classicizin' the Rock: A Selectively Annotated Discography, First Supplement**. Westport, CT: Greenwood Press, 1991. LCCN 91-7899. ISBN 0-313-27542-4. ML156.4.R6D9

Divided into three sections, the first section lists recordings of popular (or rock) arrangements of classical repertoire. The second section lists recordings of rock (or popular) songs as performed by classical artists. Both sections are arranged alphabetically by artist/ensemble. The third section contains lists detailing other connections between rock and the classics. It includes appendixes and a combined index of artists/ensembles and titles. [R: ARBA 1986, pp. 502-3; BL, Nov 15 1985, p. 477; Choice, Dec 85, p. 580; Notes, June 86, pp. 786-7 (original volume); ARBA 1992, p. 536 (supplement)]

277.   Edwards, John. **Rock 'n' Roll through 1969: Discographies of All Performers Who Hit the Charts, Beginning in 1955**. Jefferson, NC: McFarland, 1992. 380p. LCCN 91-50145. ISBN 0-89950-655-0
——. **Rock 'n' Roll, 1970 through 1979: Discographies of All Performers Who Hit the Charts**. Jefferson, NC: McFarland, 1992. 640p. LCCN 92-50887. ISBN 0-89950-768-9. ML156.4.R6E32

Each volume contains an alphabetical listing of artists/groups that had charted recordings during the periods covered. Each

entry includes personnel, album and single titles with release
dates (year only) and peak chart position. Entries include the
city or country of origin and style. It includes a name index of
all personnel. [R: ARBA 1994, p. 563 (50s/60s volume);
Choice, Nov 93, p. 430 (70s volume)]

278.   Escott, Colin and Martin Hawkins. **Sun Records: The
       Discography**. Vollersode, W. Germany: Bear Family
       Records, c1987. 240p. LCCN 93-180529. ISBN 3-924787-09-
       3. ML156.4.P6E9

       A complete discography of the Sun Record label. It is
       arranged alphabetically by artist or group. Sessions are listed
       chronologically under artist/group name and include: the
       session date, location, sidemen (when information is
       available), matrix number, song title, and issue number. This
       is followed by a listing of sun singles by matrix number that
       lists artist, title, issue number and release date. There is also
       a list of Sun EPs, as well as a list of Sun LPs. Each is
       arranged by issue number and includes the artist's name song
       titles.

279.   Furusho, Shinjiro, comp. **Riverside Jazz Records**. Chiba
       City, Japan: Shinjiro Furusho, 1984. 275p.

       Entries are divided into seven issue series. Within each divi-
       sion, entries are listed by record (or catalog) number. Entries
       include: album titles; song titles; personnel; session dates and
       cities; and master numbers. It contains an index of musicians
       which includes sidemen.

280.   Gambaccini, Paul, Tim Rice and Jonathan Rice. **British Hit
       Albums**. 5th ed. New York: Billboard/Watson-Guptill, 1992.
       416p. ISBN 0-8230-7851-5

       An alphabetically arranged list of artists and groups who had
       albums on the British charts from 1958 through 1991. The
       charts from Record Retailer, later known as Music Week, were
       used for this compilation. A brief (one line) description of each
       artist/group is included. Each album entry includes the
       release date, title, label, issue number, peak chart position,
       and the number of weeks charted. [R: ARBA 1994, p. 558]

281.   Gambaccini, Paul, Jonathan Rice and Tim Rice. **British Hit**

Singles: Every Single Hit Since 1952. 8th ed. New York: Watson-Guptill, 1991. 406p. LCCN 92-116023. ISBN 0-04-497026-9. ML156.4.P6R5

A listing of artists and groups who had singles on the British charts. It is based on the Record Retailer/Music Week charts from 1952 through 1990. Entries include title, label, issue number, release date, peak position, and the number of weeks charted.

282.   Gart, Galen and Roy Ames. **Duke-Peacock Records: An Illustrated History with Discography**. Milford, NH: Big Nickel, 1990. 234p. LCCN 91-143249. ISBN 0-936433-12-4. ML429.R6G4

More than half of this book is an informative, heavily illustrated, history of the legendary Texas record company. The remainder is a complete discography of the label and its affiliates. This is first divided by singles/LPs, then further divided by issuing label. Each singles entry includes title, artist, matrix & catalog numbers, and date (approximate - month & year only). Each LP entry includes the artist, album title and catalog number; as well as the song titles and their catalog numbers (when available). There is an artist index covering both the discography and the text. [R: Notes, Mar 93, pp. 1076-7]

283.   Ginell, Cary, comp. **The Decca Hillbilly Discography, 1927-1945**. Westport, CT: Greenwood Press, 1989. 402p. LCCN 89-17186. ISBN 0-313-26053-2. ML156.4.C7G56

A comprehensive discography of one of the most important catalogs of early country and western music. Similar to the Ruppli discographies, recordings are listed by matrix number listing personnel (when available), recording dates, and locations. It includes an artist index and a song title index. [R: ARBA 1991, p, 530; Choice June 90, p. 1654; Notes, Jun 92, pp. 1312-4; RQ, Winter 90, p. 287]

284.   Gonzalez, Fernando L. **Disco-File: The Discographical Catalog of American Rock & Roll and Rhythm & Blues, Vocal Harmony Groups, 1902-1976**. 2nd rev. ed. Flushing, NY: Gonzalez, 1977. 488p. LCCN 77-078396. ISBN 0-9601090-1-3. ML156.4.P6

A privately published discography listing more than 31,000 recordings. Arranged alphabetically by artist/group, entries include song titles, label and catalog numbers, matrix numbers, and dates. It additionally includes early gospel, barbershop, and jazz vocal groups. [R: RSR, July 1978, p. 5]

285.   Gribin, Anthony J. and Matthew M. Schiff. **Doo-Wop: The Forgotten Third of Rock 'n Roll**. Iola, WI: Krouse Publications, 1992. 612p. LCCN 91-77560. ISBN 0-87341-197-8. ML3527.G75

The first part of this book is a history of doo-wop style music and artists. It includes a number of interesting compiled lists (most recorded songs, songs by subject, etc.) as well as a list of the top 100 doo-wop recordings (according to the authors). The remainder of the text is a discography (called a songography), arranged by artist, of over 25,000 songs recorded by this style of vocal group. Entries include song titles with release dates, label, and issue number. Personnel are not listed except when a lead singers name is given to distinguish his/her recordings from another lead singer. It includes a bibliography, but no indexes. [R: ARBA 1993, p. 545; Choice, Sept 1993, p. 136; Notes, Mar 95, pp. 959-61]

286.   Harris, Steve. **Film and Television Composers: An International Discography, 1920-1989**. Jefferson, NC: McFarland & Company, c1992. LCCN 91-52637. ISBN 0-89950-553-8. ML156.4.M6H28

Al listing of film and television composers and all significant recordings of their music. The composers are listed alphabetically as are the recordings following each. Entries include titles, format, label, and issue number. A title index is included.

287.   Harris, Steve. **Film, Television and Stage Music on Phonograph Records: A Discography**. Jefferson, NC: McFarland & Company, 1988. LCCN 87-42509. ISBN 0-89950-251-2. ML156.4.M6H3

A catalog of "all important phonograph recordings of film, television and stage music from United States and Great Britain productions (Introduction)." It is divided into the three general categories. Entries are alphabetical by title and list

composer, year of production, format, label, and issue number.
It includes a composer index.

288.   Hayes, Cedric J. and Robert Laughton. **Gospel Records:
        1943-1969, A Black Music Discography**. London: Record
        Information Services, 1992. (distributed by Milford, NH: Big
        Nickel Publications) 2v. 881p.   ISBN 0-907872-28-X (v. 1; A-
        K), 0-907872-29-8 (v. 2; L-Z).

        A comprehensive discography of Gospel music singers, vocal
        groups and choirs.   It also includes Gospel and religious
        recordings made by blues, rhythm & blues, and jazz artists.
        Entries include song title, label, issue numbers, matrix
        numbers, personnel, and lead singers. There is an index of
        vocalists (individual group members) and an index of
        accompanists.

289.   Heier, Uli and Rainer E. Lotz, eds. **The Banjo on Record: A
        Bio-Discography**. Westport, CT: Greenwood Press, 1993.
        597p.   LCCN 92-38459.   ISBN 0-313-28492-X.   ISSN 0192-
        334X. ML156.4.B36B3

        A listing of records of all banjo soloists or duettists, as well as
        dance and jazz records that feature a banjo solo of significant
        length.   It is arranged alphabetically by artist with cross-
        references to pseudonyms and ensemble names.   Entries
        include the song title, recording date, recording location, label,
        matrix number, and issue number. It includes an index to all
        song titles.

290.   Hoffmann, Frank and George Albert, comps. **The Cash Box
        Country Album Charts, 1964-1988**.   Metuchen, NJ:
        Scarecrow, 1989. 290p. LCCN 89-27934. ISBN 0-8108-2273-
        3. ML156.4.C7H63

        A compilation of the Cash Box Country Album Charts over the
        25 year period. It is arranged alphabetically by artist/Group.
        Under each entry is listed all album titles (alphabetically)
        with label and catalog number, date of chart entry, number of
        weeks on the chart, and chart progress (a list of the recording's
        chart position for each week charted).   It includes an index of
        album titles. [R: ARBA 1991, P. 530; RBB, June 1 1990, p.
        1921]

291. Hoffmann, Frank and George Albert. **The Cash Box Album Charts, 1955-1974**. Metuchen, NJ: Scarecrow, 1988. 512p. LCCN 87-12716. ISBN 0-8108-2005-6
——. **The Cash Box Album Charts, 1975-1985**. Metuchen, NJ: Scarecrow, 1987. 546p. LCCN 86-31353. ISBN 0-8108-1939-2. ML156.4.P6H587

These two volumes are a compilation of all of the Cash Box album charts from 1955 through 1985. Each is arranged alphabetically by artist/group, followed by each charted album title, it's label and catalog number, the date it first charted, the number of weeks it charted, and its position number for each week that it charted. Each volume contains an album title index. [R: ARBA 1989, pp. 489-90; WLB, May 88, pp. 106,108 (1955-1974); ARBA 1988, p. 518; Notes, Mar 89, p. 520 (1975-1985)]

292. Hoffmann, Frank and George Albert. **The Cash Box Black Contemporary Album Charts, 1975-1987**. Metuchen, NJ: Scarecrow, 1989. 239p. LCCN 88-35663. ISBN 0-8108-2212-1. ML156.4.P6H589

All of the data from the Cash Box Black Contemporary Album Charts (originally called the Top R&B Album Chart), from its inception in 1975 through 1987. It is arranged by artist/group, listing each charted LP with label and catalog number, date first charted, number of weeks on the chart, and the records position each week that it charted. It includes an album title index. [R: ARBA 1990, p. 540]

293. Hoffmann, Frank and George Albert. **The Cash Box Country Singles Charts, 1958-1982**. Metuchen, NJ: Scarecrow, 1984. 596p. LCCN 84-1266. ISBN 0-8108-1685-7. ML156.4.P6A4

An index to all recordings that appeared on Cash Box (magazine) Country Singles Charts from 1958 to 1982. (The chart began in 1958 as the Country Best Sellers - Top 10 Chart, eventually growing into the Top 100 Country in 1975.) It is an alphabetical list of artists and ensembles followed by an alphabetical list of their singles. Each entry includes the song title; label; catalog number; the date that the record first appeared on the chart; the total weeks charted; and the record's number position for each week that it charted. It includes an index linking songs titles to the artist(s) that recorded them.

[R: ARBA 1985, p. 439; LJ, Aug 84, p. 1435]

294. Hoffmann, Frank. **The Cash Box Singles Charts, 1950-
      1981**. Metuchen, NJ: Scarecrow, 1983. 860p. LCCN 82-
      19126. ISBN 0-8108-1595-8. ML156.4.P6H59

      An index to all recordings that appeared on Cash Box (mag-
      azine) Top 100 Charts from 1950 to 1981. (The chart began in
      1950 as the Top 10 Chart, eventually growing into the Top 100
      in 1958.) It is an alphabetical list of artists and ensembles
      followed by an alphabetical list of their singles. Each entry
      includes the song title; record company and catalog number;
      the date that the record first appeared on the chart; the total
      weeks charted; and the record's number position for each week
      that it charted. It includes an index of songs titles. [R: ARBA
      1984, pp. 449-50; Choice, Nov 83, p. 402; LJ, Aug 83, pp. 1470-
      1; WLB, Sept 83, p. 65]

295. Hummel, David. **The Collector's Guide to the American
      Music Theater**. Metuchen, NJ: Scarecrow, 1984. 2 v. LCCN
      83-7520. ISBN 0-8108-1637-7. ML156.4.O46H85

      A guide to recordings of American musical shows. Entries are
      alphabetically arranged by show title and include composers
      and lyricists; authors; where and when the show ran; song
      titles; conductors; cast members; and record information.
      Some privately owned recordings are listed. Volume two is an
      index of all personal names listed in the entries. [R: Notes,
      Dec 86, pp. 301-3]

296. Jasen, David A. **Recorded Ragtime, 1897-1958**. Hamden,
      CT: Shoe String, 1973. 155p. LCCN 73-301. ISBN 0-208-
      01327-X. ML156.4.R25J4

      A discography of all 78 rpm flat disc ragtime recordings. It
      contains an alphabetical list of song titles with composer.
      Each entry is followed by the performers who recorded the
      song including record label and number, and recording date.
      A second section is an alphabetical list of composers followed
      by their compositions with copyright dates. An index of per-
      formers is included. [R: Notes, Sept 74, pp. 63-66]

297. Jepsen, Jorgen Grunnet.   **Jazz Records, 1942-1969**.

Copenhagen: Knudson, 1963-70. 8 vols. LCCN 77-374154.
ML156.4.J3J5

Long an essential tool of jazz researchers, this discography
picks up where Brian Rust's discography left off. It is
arranged alphabetically by artist, listing song titles, personnel, record labels, catalog and matrix numbers, and recording
dates.

298.   Kelly, Michael "Doc Rock." **Liberty Records: A history of
the Recording Company and Its Stars, 1955-1971**.
Jefferson, NC: McFarland, 1992.   592p.   LCCN 92-50307.
ISBN 0-89950-740-9. ML3790.K44

Though primarily a history of the record label, this book also
contains important discographical information. Part one is a
year-by-year account of the label's major successes - focusing
on the artists. Part two focuses on the people that worked
behind-the-scenes (engineers, producers, sales managers, etc.).
Part three is a more in-depth look at Liberty's four major acts.
The appendices include lists of "top" recordings and artists, as
well as a complete lists of singles and LPs, arranged by matrix
number. It includes an index of names and song titles.

299.   Kiner, Larry F. and Harry Mackenzie.   **Basic Musical
Library, "P" Series, 1-1000**. New York: Greenwood Press,
1990.   326p. (Discographies, number 39.) LCCN 90-40207.
ISBN 0-313-27527-0. ML156.4.P6K56

A guide to the popular music transcriptions issued by the
Armed Forces Radio Service, beginning in the early 1940s.
These were 16 inch 33 1/3 discs (about 28 minutes long)
designed to be complete radio shows and distributed to U.S.
military installations worldwide. The individual tracks were
copied from recordings of studio broadcasts, radio show
rehearsals, commercial recordings, and alternate studio takes.
The first 1,000 transcriptions are included here, each listing
the catalog number and issue number. Track information
includes the artist, song title, running time, and source of
track when known. There is an index of artists and an index
of song titles.

300.   Laing, Ralph and Chris Sheridan, comps. **Jazz Records: The
Specialist Labels**. Copenhagen: Jazzmedia, c1981.   2 v.

ISBN 87-88043-00-2. ML156.4.J3L26

A guide to the recordings released by independent jazz labels
not covered in the Brian Rust or Jorgan Jepsen discographies.
Entries are arranged alphabet by label (more than 130 labels
are covered), and include catalog number, title, artist, personnel, recording dates (many entries are reissues), and song
titles. The lack of indexes makes this difficult to use as reference tool.

301.   Leadbitter, Mike and Neil Slaven. **Blues Records, January
        1943 to December 1966**. New York: Oak Publications, 1968.
        381p.   LCCN 78-313461.   ISBN 0-907872-07-7 (2d ed.).
        ML156.4.J3L4

        A selective discography intended for the blues record collector.
        Entries are arranged alphabetically by artist and include song
        titles, personnel, record labels, catalog and matrix numbers,
        and recording dates (when available). Volume one, A through
        K, of a second edition is published by Big Nickel, 1987. [R:
        Notes, June 70, pp. 556-8]

302.   Leder, Jan, comp.   **Women in Jazz: A Discography of
        Instrumentalists, 1913-1968**.   Westport, CT: Greenwood
        Press, 1985. 305p. LCCN 85-17657. ISBN 0-313-24790-0.
        ML156.4.J3L44

        An alphabetically arranged discography of women jazz instru-
        mentalists.   Entries are arranged chronologically under the
        artist and include song titles, personnel, record labels, catalog
        and matrix numbers, and recording dates.   There is also a
        section of jazz collections which include women artists and an
        artist index that cross-references both sections.   [R: ARBA
        1986, p. 494]

303.   Lord, Tom. **The Jazz Discography**. West Vancouver, BC:
        Lord Music Reference, 1992. distributed by Redwood, NY:
        North Country. v.1 A-Bankhead; v. 2 Banks-Boustedt; v.3
        Boutte-Cathcart, ISBN 1-881993-02-7; v.4 Catherine-Dagradi,
        ISBN 1-881993-03-5; v.5 Dahlander-Dutch Dixie Devils, ISBN
        1-881993-04-3; v.6 Dutch Swing College Band-Fischbacher,
        ISBN 1-881993-05-1; v.7 Fischer-Gonda, ISBN 1-881993-06-X;
        v.8 Gonella-Harp, LCCN 93-235534,   ISBN 1-881993-07-8.
        ML156.4.J3 L67

A very comprehensive discography of jazz covering from 1898 into the 1990s. It covers all styles of jazz: traditional, swing, bebop, modern, avant-garde, fusion, third stream, etc. It is projected to include more than 100,000 recordings, in 25 volumes, when complete. Both a musicians index and a song title index are projected to be included. Entries are listed under leader or group name, chronologically by session date. Under each session is listed the place of recording, personnel, label, matrix numbers, and catalog numbers. Album titles are indicated when appropriate. [R: ARBA 193, p. 545; Choice, Apr 93, p. 1297]

304.   Lotz, Rainer E. & Ulrich Neuert.   **The AFRS "Jubilee" Transcription Programs, an Exploratory Discography**. 2v. Frankfurt, Germany: Norbert Ruecker, 1985. ISBN 3-923397-01-1

The Jubilee transcription programs were a series of radio programs intended for Black U.S. servicemen during World War II and briefly after. They featured live performances of some of the most significant jazz musicians of the period. This is a discography of that series. Each entry includes program and catalog numbers, date of dubbing, artists, song titles, and sidemen (when information is available). It includes an artist index and a song title index.

305.   Lynch, Richard C., comp.   **Broadway on Record: A Directory of New York Cast Recordings of Musical Shows, 1931-1986**. Westport, CT: Greenwood Press, 1987. 357p. LCCN 87-11822. ISBN 0-313-25523-7. ML156.4.O46L9

A discography of commercially available original cast recordings of popular Broadway and off-Broadway musical productions. Entries are listed alphabetically by show title and include: opening date and theatre; label and catalog number; composers and authors, cast and song titles. It includes a chronological list of productions, as well as a performer index and a technical (composers, lyricists, etc.) index. [R: Choice, Jan 91, p. 760]

306.   Lynch, Richard C., comp.   **Movie Musicals on Record: A Directory of Recordings of Motion Picture Musicals, 1927-1987**. Westport, CT: Greenwood Press, 1989.   455p. LCCN 89-2137. ISBN 0-313-26540-2. ML156.4.M6L9

A listing of commercially available original cast recordings of movie musicals. Entries are listed alphabetically by movie title and include: release date; record label and catalog number; composer/lyricist, musical director, cast and song titles. It included is a chronological list of productions, as well as a performer index and a technical (composers, lyricists, etc.) index. [R: ARBA 1990, pp. 523-4; Choice, Dec 89, p. 613; LJ, Nov 1 1989, p. 84; RBB, Dec 151989, pp. 856-7; RQ, Winter 89, pp. 296-7]

307. Lynch, Richard C., comp. **TV and Studio Cast Musicals on Record: A Discography of Television Musicals and Stage Recordings**. Westport, CT: Greenwood Press, 1990. 330p. ISBN 0-313-27324-3. ML156.4.046L93

A discography of commercial recordings of television musicals and studio cast recordings of stage and film musicals. It is intended to compliment two previously published books (Broadway on Record, and Movie Musicals on Record), each listing only original cast recordings. Entries are listed alphabetically by title and include dates, label and catalog number, writers, cast, and song titles. It includes a chronologies of television, studio cast, and movie musical titles; a performer index; and a technical index (composers, lyricists and directors). [R: ARBA 1991, p. 533]

308. Mackenzie, Harry and Lothar Polomski, comps. **One Night Stand Series, 1-1001**. New York: Greenwood Press, 1991. (Discographies no. 44.) 394p. LCCN 91-7317. ISBN 0-313-27729-X. ML156.4.P6M253

A guide to the live recorded performance transcription series issued by the Armed Forces Radio Service. These were edited for military broadcasts and issued on 16 inch 33 1/3 rpm discs (about 15 minutes per side). Most were transcribed from commercial broadcasts. The series began in 1943 and featured popular artists (most are big bands, though some recordings feature popular ethnic music). The entries are listed chronologically by issue number. Each entry includes the artists (including vocalists when appropriate), the location and date of the performance, the song titles and brief performance notes. It is indexed by performer/band leader.

309. Mawhinney, Paul C. **The MusicMaster: The 45 RPM**

Record Directory by Artist. Pittsburgh, PA: Record-Rama Sound Archives, 1983. ISBN 0-910925-00-3

———. **The MusicMaster: The 45 RPM Record Directory by Title**. Pittsburgh, PA: Record-Rama Sound Archives, 1983. ISBN 0-910925-01-1

———. **MusicMaster: The 45 RPM Singles Directory/Supplement: 44 Years of Recorded Music, 1948-1992: Alphabetically Listed by Artist**. Pittsburgh, PA: Record-Rama Sound Archives, c1992. LCCN 93-194413. ISBN 0-910925-03-8

———. **MusicMaster: The 45 RPM Singles Directory/Supplement: 44 Years of Recorded Music, 1948-1992: Alphabetically Listed by Title**. Pittsburgh, PA: Record-Rama Sound Archives, c1992. LCCN 93-194427. ISBN 0-910925-04-6. ML156.4.P6M9

A comprehensive listing of nearly 100,000 45 rpm records released between 1947 and 1982. Every known recording by any established artist, and any version of a standard or classic song title is listed. This is more than twice the number of recorded singles that have appeared on the Billboard charts. Entries include: artist(s), song title, label, manufacturer number, and year of release. [R: Notes, Mar 84, pp. 547-50]

310. McAleer, Dave. **The All Music Book of Hit Singles: Top Twenty Charts from 1954 to the Present Day**. San Francisco: Miller Freeman, 1994. 431 p. LCCN 94-11272. ML156.4.P6M42

A month-by-month listing, beginning January 1954 through December 1993, of the top 20 U.S. and British singles. The U.S. charts are derived from Billboard Magazine's weekly charts, while the British charts are based on New Music Express' (before 1964) and Record Retailer/Music Week charts. Each entry includes title, artist, label, number of weeks in the top 20. Entries also indicate gold or platinum status (sales over 1 million or 2 million respectively) and if the single was the artists' first or last top 20 hit. Brief descriptions of significant popular music events are included throughout the book. There is an artist index and a song title index.

311. McAleer, Dave. **The Omnibus Book of British and American Hit Singles, 1960-1990**. London: Omnibus Press (distributed by New York: Music Sales), c1990. 160p. ISBN 0-7119-2180-6. ML156.4.P6M32

A listing of all single recordings that have reached the top 10 positions in the UK and USA. Entries are arranged alphabetically by artist/group and include brief biographies or profiles.

312. Miletich, Leo N. **Broadway's Prize-Winning Musicals: An Annotated Guide for Libraries and Audio Collectors**. Binghamton, NY: Haworth Press, 1993. LCCN 92-4125. ISBN 1-56024-288-4. ML156.4.M8M54

A guide to musical theater productions that were awarded a Tony Award, New York Drama Critics Circle Award, Pulitzer Prize, and/or Grammy Award. Shows are listed chronologically under each award. Entries include title, writers, opening date, cast members, song titles, plot summary and production notes. Each entry also includes the label and issue number of the original cast album. The author also includes a number of entries for notable musicals that did not receive awards. The general index includes names and show titles.

313. Muirhead, Bert. **The Record Producers File: A Directory of Rock Album Producers 1962-1984**. Poole, England: Blandford Press, 1984. 288p. ISBN 0-7137-1429-8; 0-7137-1430-1 (pbk.). ML3534.M9

An alphabetical listing of record producers and the albums they produced. The recording artist, album title, record label, and release date (year) is listed for each of the 20,000-plus titles listed. Albums are limited to those listed in British or U.S. record charts. Compilation, or "best of...", albums are excluded. Also excluded are self-produced recordings, unless the artist has produced a significant number of recordings of other artists. It includes an index of artist and ensemble names. [R: ARBA 1986, pp. 504-5; RBB, July 85, p. 1525]

314. Raben, Erik. **Jazz Records, 1942-1980**. Copenhagen: Jazzmedia, 1987[?]. vol. 1 A-Ba, ISBN 87-88043-06-1; vol. 2 Bar-Br, ISBN 87-88043-09-6; vol. 3 Bro-Cl; Vol. 6 Duke Ellington (by Ole J. Nielson), ISBN 87-88043-14-2. ML156.4.J3J47

A comprehensive discography of recorded jazz, intended to supplant Jepsen's monumental work. Volumes have been issued periodically. Entries include song titles, label, issue numbers, matrix numbers, personnel, recording date, and location. Each volume includes an index of personnel.

315.   Rogers, Alice. **Dance Bands & Big Bands: Documenting Over 30,000 Golden Age Dance & Big Band Recordings-- All on 78 rpm Singles**. Tempe, AZ: Jellyroll Productions, c1986. 173p. LCCN 85-62141. ML156.4.B5R6

A discography of dance band recordings from the turn of the century to the 1950s, although most were released in the 1920s through the 1940s. Nearly 16,000 records are listed. Entries are alphabetical; first by artist then by (A side) song title. Each entry includes song titles of both sides, the label, release number, year of issue and vocalist's name (if known).

316.   Ruppli, Michel and Bob Porter, comps. **The Savoy Label: A Discography**. Westport, CT: Greenwood Press, 1980. 442p. (Discographies, no. 2; ISSN 0192-334X) LCCN 79-7727. ISBN 0-313-21199-X. ML156.2.R787

A listing of all recordings made or issued by Savoy Records. Listed in a rough chronological sequence (by master number), part one lists all Savoy sessions, while part two lists all sessions purchased or leased by Savoy. Part three lists all singles by record number while part four lists albums by record number. Each entry includes the artist's name; the album title (when appropriate); the sidemen and the instruments they played (when information is available); the session date; and song titles and issue numbers. The index lists the major (main entry) artists including references to sessions where they are sidemen. Other sidemen are not listed.   [R: ARBA 1981, p. 457]

317.   Ruppli, Michel and Ed Novitsky. **The Mercury Labels: A Discography**. Westport, CT: Greenwood Press, 1993. 5v. (Discographies, no. 51; ISSN 0192-334X)   LCCN 93-15254. ISBN 0-313-27371-5. ML156.2.R7853

A comprehensive discography of the Mercury label and its subsidiaries. Volume one through four are divided chronologically (v.1, 1945-1956; v.2, 1956-1964; v.3, 1964-1969; v.4, 1969-1991) with entries arranged by session. Each entry includes artist/group name, musicians, date, location, song titles,

matrix numbers and catalog numbers. Volume five lists
singles, albums and compact discs by catalog numbers, and
includes a general artist index.

318.   Ruppli, Michel, comp.   **The Aladdin/Imperial Labels: A
       Discography**. Westport, CT: Greenwood Press, 1991. 727p.
       (Discographies, no. 42; ISSN 0192-334X)   LCCN 90-22696.
       ISBN 0-313-27821-0. ML156.2.R778

       This discography is divided into six sections: (1) the Alladin
       sessions, (2) the Imperial Folk/Dance sessions, (3) the Imperial
       popular sessions, (4) additional leased and purchased sessions,
       (5) single numerical listings, and (6) album numerical listings.
       There is an artist index, listing both leaders and sidemen.
       Entries, like the author's other works, include the artist's
       name; the album title (when appropriate); the sidemen and
       the instruments they played (when information is available);
       the session date; the song titles; and issue/matrix numbers.
       [R: ARBA 1992, p. 530; Notes, Mar 93, pp. 1077-8]

319.   Ruppli, Michel, comp.   **Atlantic Records: A Discography**.
       Westport, CT: Greenwood Press, 1979.   4 v. (Discographies,
       no. 1; ISSN 0192-334X)   LCCN 78-75237.   ISBN 0-313-21170-
       X. ML156.2.R78

       A listing of all Atlantic Records recording sessions through
       1978. Listings are by master (or matrix) number and are, for
       the most part, chronological.   Recordings released but not
       produced by Atlantic are included in each volume.   Each entry
       includes the artist's name; the album title (when appropriate);
       the sidemen and the instruments they played (when informa-
       tion is available); the session date; and song titles and issue
       numbers. Volume one through three each contain an index of
       the major artists included in that volume.   Volume four con-
       tains a compiled index of major artists from all four volumes.
       [R: ARBA 1980, p. 432; LJ, Nov 15, 1979, p. 2447; Notes, Sept
       80, pp. 63-4]

320.   Ruppli, Michel, comp.   **The Chess Labels: A Discography**.
       Westport, CT: Greenwood Press, 1983.   2 v. (Discographies,
       no. 7; ISSN 0192-334X)   LCCN 82-25148.   ISBN 0-313-23471-
       X. ML156.2.R783

       A discography of the various record labels managed by
       Leonard and Phil Chess from 1947.   Part one lists all Chess

(brothers) recordings. Part two lists recordings made after the Chess label(s) and catalog were sold to GRT. These are listed by master (matrix) number and are in a rough chronological order. Parts three and four list singles and albums by record (catalog) number. Each entry includes the artist's name; the album title (when appropriate); the sidemen and the instruments they played (when information is available); the session date; and song titles and issue numbers. The index includes all artists listed in the entries. [R: ARBA 1984, pp. 443-4; LJ, Sept 1 1983, p. 1698; Notes, June 84, pp. 791-2]

321.   Ruppli, Michel, comp.   **The Cleff/Verve Labels: A Discography**. New York: Greenwood Press, 1986. 2 vols. (Discographies, no. 26; ISSN 0192-334X) LCCN 86-19530. ISBN 0-313-25294-7. ML156.2.R784

A discographical listing of all recordings issued by the Clef and Verve labels and their subsidiaries. Entries are listed by matrix numbers which, by their organization, divides the discography by labels, series an type; and also keeps each area in chronological order. Entries include song titles, personnel, catalog and matrix numbers, and session dates. It includes an index of all musicians listed. [R: ARBA 1988, p. 512]

322.   Ruppli, Michel, comp. **The Prestige Label: A Discography**. Westport, CT: Greenwood Press, 1980. 377p. (Discographies, no. 3; ISSN 0192-334X) LCCN 79-8294. ISBN 0-313-22019-0. ML156.2.R786

A guide to all Prestige Label recordings. Part one is devoted to Prestige sessions while part 2 lists sessions purchased or leased from other labels or producers. Part three is a numerical listing of singles while part four is a numerical listing of albums. Entries list song titles, location and date, personnel, and matrix/issue numbers. There is an artist index, listing both leaders and sidemen. [R: ARBA 1981, pp. 456-7]

323.   Ruppli, Michel.   **The King Labels: A Discography**. Westport CT: Greenwood Press, 1985. 2 v. (Discographies, no. 18; ISSN 0192-334X) LCCN 85-17655. ISBN 0-313-24771-4. ML156.2.R785

A discography of the King record label, it's subsidiary labels, and labels exclusively distributed by King. These are first

listed by master series number and include song titles, personnel, recording dates and issue numbers. This is followed by a
list of singles releases and a list of album releases both with
references to the session information. The index includes all
artists listed in the entries. [R: ARBA 1986, p. 484]

324. Rust, Brian and Allen Debus. **The Complete
      Entertainment Discography: From 1892 to 1942**. 2nd ed.
      New York: Da Capo, 1989. [1st ed. - New Rochelle, NY:
      Arlington House, 1973.] 794p. LCCN 87-33155. ISBN 0-306-
      76210-2. ML156.4.P6R88

      A discography of all known recordings of the period excluding
      jazz and blues artists, and music of commercial dance bands.
      Essentially, this volume fills in the gap left by the author's
      other discographies. Included are commercial singers, as well
      as minstrel pioneers, vaudevillians, and film and radio person-
      alities.   The entries are listed alphabetically by artist and
      include song titles, personnel (when available), record labels,
      catalog and matrix numbers, and recording dates

325. Rust, Brian, comp. **Jazz Records, 1897-1942**. 4th enlarged
      ed. New York, Arlington House, 1978. 2 vols. LCCN 78-1693.
      ISBN 0-87000-404-2. ML156.4.J3R9

      The essential discographic tool for jazz recordings through
      1942. It is arranged alphabetically by artist, listing song
      titles, personnel, record labels, catalog and matrix numbers,
      and recording dates. It includes an index of all musicians
      listed and an index of song titles. [R: ARBA 1979, pp. 488-9;
      Choice, Nov 78, p. 1196; LJ, Oct 1 1978, p. 1970; Notes, Mar
      79, p. 638]

326. Rust, Brian. **The American Dance Band Discography:
      1917-1942**. New Rochelle, NY: Arlington House, 1975. LCCN
      75-33689. ISBN 0-87000-248-1. ML156.4.P6R87

      A discography of recorded dance (or popular) music, covering
      ensembles not listed in Jazz Records: 1987-1942. It is
      arranged alphabetically by artist, listing song titles, person-
      nel, record labels, catalog and matrix numbers, and recording
      dates. It includes an index of all musicians listed and an
      index of song titles. [R: ARBA 1976, pp. 475-6; Notes, June
      76, p. 782; Notes, Dec 77, pp. 293-4]

327.   Ryan, Marc. **Trumpet Records: An Illustrated History
        with Discography**. Milford, NH: Big Nickel, 1992. 114p.
        ISBN 0936433-14-0

Trumpet Records was a small, family owned record company
in Jackson Mississippi. Between 1950 and 1956 they recorded
blues country and gospel artists. The major portion of this
book is a well illustrated history of the company but it also
includes a complete discography of the Trumpet (and Globe)
label.   The discography is a chronological list of all
Trumpet/Globe sessions.   Each entry includes the artist's
name; the sidemen and the instruments they played; the
session date; and song titles with issue and matrix numbers.
The index includes both the history and the discography.

328.   Scheffner, Manfred. **Bielefelder Katalog: Jazz**. Stuttgart,
        Germany, 1959-1991. Annual, ISSN 0721-7153

An international trade catalog of jazz LPs, CDs, and cassettes
in print. It is divided into three sections: (1) the title index
lists all song titles and the recordings on which they appear;
(2) the artist index links all sidemen to the recordings on
which they appear; and (3) the label index lists, by record
company and catalog number, all of the records indexed with
full discographical information.

329.   Sears, Richard S. **V-Discs: A History and Discography**.
        Westport, CT: Greenwood Press, 1980. 1166p. (Discographies,
        No. 5) LCCN 80-1022. ISBN 0-313-22207-X
        ———.   **V-Discs: First Supplement**.   Westport, CT:
        Greenwood Press, 1986. 300p. (Discographies, No. 5) LCCN
        86-19529. ISBN 0-313- 25421-4. ML156.2.S44

V-discs were recordings produced during and immediately following World War II. They were produced by the U.S. military, for the military. Most were transcriptions of popular
recordings of the time, others were unique recordings produced for the series, still others were unique unissued commercial recordings or broadcasts. This discography lists these
recordings alphabetically by artist with thorough annotations
(dates, personnel, etc.). The supplement corrects errors and
adds 600 new items discovered since the initial volume. [R:
ARBA 1982, p. 512; BL, Sept 1 1981, p. 69; Choice, May 81,
p1242 (original volume); ARBA 1988, p. 513 (suppl.)]

330.   Smith, Charles Edward, et al. **The Jazz Record Book**. New
        York: Smith & Durrell, 1942. 515p. (Reprinted by Scholarly
        Press) LCCN 72-181261. ISBN 0-403-01684-3. ML156.4.J355

        The first section of this book is a history of jazz divided into
        five sections: (1) Chicago breakdown; (2) New York and
        Harlem; (3) blues and boogie woogie; (4) seven brass, four reed;
        and (5) they still play jazz. Part two is an annotated discogra-
        phy divided under the same headings. Entries list record
        labels, record numbers and personnel. It includes an artist
        index.

331.   Stagg, Tom and Charlie Crump, comps. **New Orleans: The
        Revival**. [?]: Bashall Eaves, 1973. 307p. ISBN 0-902-638-
        017. ML156.4.J3S8

        "A tape and discography of Negro traditional jazz recorded in
        New Orleans or by New Orleans Bands 1937-1972" (from the
        title page). It is arranged alphabetically by major artist fol-
        lowed by the group name. Entries list song titles, session
        dates, personnel, and record numbers when available.

132.   Walters, David. **The Children of Nuggets: The Definitive
        Guide to "Psychedelic Sixties" Punk Rock on
        Compilation Albums**. Ann Arbor, MI: Popular Culture Ink,
        1990. 372p. LCCN 89-92331. ISBN 0-8240-4447-9.
        ML156.4.R6W34

        An index to compilation albums of "pre-punk" sixties artists
        and bands. This includes psychedelic and garage bands - any
        music with a rough-edged sound. More than 300 albums are
        listed with complete song title selections, each assigned a
        unique number for indexing. The albums are then indexed by
        artist/group, followed by an index by song title. [R: ARBA
        1991, p. 537; Choice, Sept 90, pp. 84-6]

333.   Whitburn, Joel. **The Billboard Book of Top 40 Albums**.
        rev. ed. New York: Billboard Books/Watson-Guptill, 1991.
        347p. LCCN 90-22777. ISBN 0-8230-7534-6 (pbk.).
        ML156.4.P6W43

        A listing of all albums that reached the top 40 positions in the
        Billboard album charts from 1955 through 1990. It is
        arranged alphabetically by the artist/group, under which

albums are listed chronologically. Each album entry includes
title, label and issue number, date charted, number of weeks
charted, and peak chart position. This is essentially an
abridged paperback version of Top Pop Albums. [R: ARBA
1992, p. 528]

334. Whitburn, Joel. **The Billboard Book of Top 40 Hits**. 4th
ed. New York: Billboard Books, 1989. 622p. LCCN 89-9706.
ISBN 0-85112-430-5. ML156.4.P6W44

A listing of every single recording that reached the top forty
positions of the Billboard Hot 100 Charts. Essentially, it is an
abridged version of Top Pop Singles, arranged alphabetically
by artist/ensemble. Under each artist, the recordings are
listed chronologically with label and record number, release
date, number of weeks charted, and peak chart position. [R:
ARBA 1984, p. 444; Choice Dec 83, p. 559; LJ, Nov 15 1983,
p. 2152 (1st edition)]

335. Whitburn, Joel. **Billboard Top 3000 Plus: 1955-1990**.
Menonomee Falls, WI: Record Research, Inc., 1990. 178p.
LCCN 89-133087. ISBN 0-89820-054-7. ML156.4.P6W457

A listing of all single recordings that charted in the top ten in
Billboard Magazine. Entries are divided by peak chart position - all number one songs are first. These are further
divided by number of weeks at peak position. (Hound
Dog/Don't be cruel is listed first since it held the number one
position for 12 weeks.) Each entry includes title, artist,
running time, number of weeks charted, number of weeks in
top 40, and number of weeks in top 10. It includes an artist
index and a title index.

336. Whitburn, Joel. **Billboard's Top Ten Charts: A Week by
Week History of the Hottest of the Hot 100, 1958-1988**.
Menonomee Falls, WI: Record Research, Inc., 1988. 600p.
ISBN 0-89820-067-9. ML156.4.P6W458

A compilation of the top 10 single recordings listed in
Billboard magazine's Hot 100 charts from August 4, 1958
through 1988. Each entry includes the artist, label and
number, the previous weeks position, and the number of
weeks charted. Also listed, under each week, is the record

that debuted at the highest position, as well as the record that advanced the most positions on the Hot 100 chart.

337. Whitburn, Joel. **Bubbling Under the Hot One Hundred, 1959-1985**. Menonomee Falls, WI: Record Research, Inc., 1988. 384p. ML156.4.P6J6

A compilation of Billboard Magazine's weekly chart that lists songs that almost make the Hot 100 chart. It includes a table, by artist, of all songs that subsequently moved on to the Hot 100. Song titles are indexed.

338. Whitburn, Joel. **Pop Memories 1890-1954: The History of American Popular Music**. Menomonee Falls, WI : Record Research Inc., 1986. 660p. ISBN 0-89820-083-0. ML156.4.P6W485

An alphabetical list of performers with a list of their most popular recordings. Some very brief biographic information is included for each artist and group. It includes an index of all of the song titles with references to artists and release dates. The data for Pop Memories, after 1920, is from Billboard Magazine. Information previous to 1920 comes from the magazines The Phonoscope, The Phonogram and Talking Machine World, as well as sheet music sales and ASCAP play lists.

339. Whitburn, Joel. **Pop Singles Annual, 1955-1990**. Menomonee Falls, WI: Record Research, Inc., 1991. 736p. ISBN 0-89820-086-5

A guide to every song listed in Billboard Magazine's singles charts since 1955. It contains two major sections. The main body is first divided by year, then subdivided by chart position in ascending order (Therefore, the first listings are the songs to reach number one in 1955, followed by the songs that peaked at number two in 1955 - and so on). Each entry includes record label, issue number, the number of weeks charted and the date that it reached its peak position. It includes an index of all of the song titles with references to artists, peak position, and year. New editions are released about every four years.

340. Whitburn, Joel. **Top Country Singles 1944-1993**. Menomonee Falls, WI: Record Research, Inc., 1994. 603p.

LCCN 94-182956. ISBN 0-89820-100-4. ML156.4.C7W5

An alphabetical listing, by artist, of every record to hit
Billboard's Country Singles charts from 1942 through 1993.
Most entries include brief biographical sketches. Recordings
are listed chronologically (under the artist) and include: the
label and record number; the date that the record was first
charted; the peak chart position that the recording reached;
and the total number of weeks that the record remained on the
charts. It includes an index of all song titles listed in the main
body.

341.   Whitburn, Joel.   **Top Pop Album Tracks 1955-1992**.
       Menomonee Falls, WI: Record Research Inc., 1992. 500p.

       A companion book to Top Pop Albums (see below), this is an
       index of all the songs from each of the albums charted in
       Billboard Magazine during the time period indicated. Over
       200,000 tracks are listed. Under each song title is listed the
       artist(s) that recorded it with the release date.

342.   Whitburn, Joel. **Top Pop Albums 1955-1992**. Menomonee
       Falls, WI: Record Research Inc., 1992. 900p.

       An index to all albums charted by Billboard magazine from
       January 1, 1955 through July 4, 1992. It is an alphabetical
       listing of artists and ensembles followed by a brief biography
       and a chronological list of album titles. Each album entry
       includes: the label and record number; the date that the record
       was first charted; the peak chart position the recording
       reached; the total number of weeks that the record remained
       on the charts; RIAA gold/platinum certification; and a com-
       plete track listing (song titles) for each album listed.
       Recordings that cannot be listed by artist are listed under
       categories (soundtracks, aerobics, comedy, etc.).

343.   Whitburn, Joel. **Top Pop Singles 1955-1990**. Menomonee
       Falls, WI: Record Research Inc., 1991. 848p. ISBN 0-89820-
       088-1

       An index to every song listed in Billboard Magazine's singles
       charts since 1955. It contains two major sections. The first is
       an alphabetical list of performers with a list of their recordings
       (with record label, catalog numbers, release date, and peak

chart position). Most entries also include some brief biographic information. The second section is an index of all of the song titles with references to artists and release dates. New editions are released about every four years.

344.   Whitburn, Joel. **Top R&B Singles 1942-1988**. Menomonee Falls, WI: Record Research Inc., 1989. 613p. ISBN 0-89820-068-7

An alphabetically list of all artists/ensembles whose records were listed in the R&B Charts of Billboard magazine between 10/24/42 and 7/2/88. Each charted record is listed chronologically (under the artist/ensemble) and includes: the label and issue number; the date that the record was first charted; the peak chart position the recording reached; and the total number of weeks that the record remained on the charts. All song titles listed are included in the index.

Critical Discographies

345. Allen, Bob. **The Blackwell Guide to Recorded Country Music**. Cambridge, MA: Blackwell, 1994. 411p. LCCN 93-44462. ISBN 0-631-19106-2. ML128.R6L49

An annotated buying guide to country music. It is divided into 10 styles (Honky Tonk, Bluegrass, etc.) or eras (the 1950 & 1960s, etc.). Each category offers a critical overview followed by specific discographical information. LPs, cassettes and compact discs are covered - many reissues. Entries include title, artist, label, issue number, and song titles. The general index lists album titles, song titles and artists. [R: LJ July 1994, p. 82]

346. **Best Rated CDs: Jazz, Popular, etc., 1992**. Voorheesville, NY: Peri Press, 1992. 678p. ISBN 1-879796-06-6

A compilation of more than 2,000 top rated CDs from *CD Review Digest-Jazz, Popular, Etc.* from 1982 to 1991. Recordings were selected that (1) were noticed by at least two reviewers and (2) received an award for excellence from at least one of these (critics choice awards, best of the year awards, etc.). Entries are divided into four broad areas: Blues, Jazz, Pop/Rock/Roots, and Show Music. Each entry includes album title, label and/or catalog number, release or session date, and total playing time. Most entries include song titles, personnel and SPARS code. It includes review citations, featuring quotes, as well as award information, are included in each entry. An artist index, which lists both leaders and sidemen, is included. [R: ARBA 1993, p. 540; RBB, Oct 1 1992, pp. 351-64]

347.   Callahan, Mike. **A Guide to Oldies on Compact Disc**.
        Fairfax Station, VA: Both Sides Now, 1991. 254p. LCCN 91-
        073288. ML156.4.P6C26

        A guide to rock era reissues compiled from the quarterly Both
        Sides Now Stereo Newsletter. It contains listings for more
        than 2,000 CD recordings. It is divided into two sections the
        first listing recordings by artist, the second listing compila-
        tions by title. Each entry lists label, catalog number, SPARS
        code, date of reissue, total timing, song titles, stereo informa-
        tion, and a rating (A, B, C, or D) of the recording's relative
        sound quality.

348.   Christgau, Robert. **Rock Albums of the '70s: A Critical
        Guide**. New York: Da Capo, 1981. LCCN 81-1977. ISBN 0-
        306-80409-3
        ——. **Christgau's Record Guide: Rock Albums of the 80s**.
        New York: Pantheon, 1990. 512p. LCCN 90-52512. ISBN 0-
        679-73015-X. ML156.9.C533

        The 1970s volume is a critical guide to nearly 3,000 popular
        albums released during the 1970s. It is arranged alphabetical-
        ly by artist/ensemble. Each entry includes a brief annotation
        and a grade (A+ down to E-). The 1980s volume follows the
        same format as the first. The criticisms are subjective with
        little technical or historical justifications. [R: ARBA 1982, p.
        524-5; BL, Oct 15, 1981, p. 276; LJ, Nov 1, 1981, p. 2126 (the
        70s guide)]

349.   DeCurtis, Anthony, James Henke and Holly George Warren.
        **The New Rolling Stone Album Guide: Completely New
        Reviews, Every Essential Album, Every Essential Artist**.
        3rd ed. New York: Random House, 1992. 838p. LCCN 92-
        50156. ISBN 0-679-73729-4. ML156.4.P6R62

        A critical guide to rock, pop, soul, country, blues, folk and
        gospel albums. It is arranged alphabetically by artist or
        ensemble, followed by a chronological list of album titles with
        label and release date. Each album is given a "star rating"
        (five stars being the best) and a brief critical annotation of the
        artist's recordings is included. [R: ARBA 1994, p. 560; BR,
        Mar/Apr 1993, p. 34; Choice Jul/Aug 1993, p. 1743]

350.   Downey, Pat. **Top 40 Music on Compact Disc, 1955-1981**.

Englewood, CO: Libraries Unlimited, 1994. LCCN 94-29740. ISBN 1-563-08307-8. ML156.4.P6D695

A guide to locating CD issues (or reissues) of top 40 records. It is arranged by artist or group and entries include song title, label, issue number, running time, peak chart position and the number of weeks charted. Chart information is based on Cash Box Magazine's Singles Charts.

351.   Eddy, Chuck. **Stairway to Hell: The 500 Best Heavy Metal Albums in the Universe**. New York: Harmony Books, 1991.   LCCN   90-47516.   ISBN   0-517-57541-8. ML156.4.R6E3

A very subjective, and sometimes outrageous, critical listing of heavy metal recordings, beginning with the best and working its way down through the top 500. Each entry is annotated and includes record label and year of release. It includes an album title index. [R: Notes, Dec 92, pp. 625-6]

352.   Erlewine, Michael, Scott Bultman and Stephen Thomas Erlewine. **All Music Guide: The Best CDs, Albums and Tapes**. San Francisco: Miller Freeman, 1992. 1176p. LCCN 92-60948. ISBN 0-87930-264-X

An ambitious guide to all recorded music. It lists over 25,000 recordings by more than 6,000 artists and groups. Entries are divided into 23 style/categories. In each category, entries are listed alphabetically by artist or group, except classical recordings (a relatively small portion of the book) which are listed by composer. Most entries include a brief biography of the performer or composer. Record entries list title, date, label, issue number, and usually a brief critical annotation. It includes an index of names.
    This book is also available electronically: (1) on CD-ROM for IBM compatible from Selectware Technology, (2) on discs for the Macintosh from Great Bear Technologies, and (3) on Compuserve and the Internet.   [R: Choice, Jul/Aug 93, p. 1743; RBB, Feb 1 93, p. 1000]

353.   Fox, Charles, et al. **Jazz on Record: A Critical Guide**. London: Hutchinson, 1960.   Reprinted by Westport, CT: Greenwood Press, 1978.   352p.   ISBN   0-313-20513-2. ML156.4.J3F7

Intended for the jazz record collector, this discography offers a selective, alphabetically arranged, list of jazz artists, each with a brief career biography and a list of available LP recordings. It includes a name index that cross-references the sidemen.

354.   Ganzl, Kurt, ed. **The Blackwell Guide to Musical Theatre on Record**. Cambridge, MA: Blackwell, 1990. 547p. LCCN 89-78226. ISBN 0-631-16517-7. ML156.9.G36

A critical guide to recordings of musicals and operettas produced for release on LPs (about the last 40 years). It is arranged chronologically in ten chapters; each offering a narrative overview of both the music and the available recordings. This is followed by a discography of recommended recordings, with ten essential recordings selected by the author. The discography entries include title, selected cast, label and issue numbers. Recordings issued or reissued on CD are designated. The index lists titles and names.

355.   Hadley, Frank J. **The Grove Press Guide to the Blues on CD**. New York: Grove Press, 1992. 309p. LCCN 92-17305. ISBN 0-8021-3328-2. ML156.4.B6H3

A guide to blues recordings available on compact discs. It includes reissues of classic performances, as well as new issues of contemporary recording artists. It is arranged alphabetically by artist, followed by compilations arranged by title. Each entry lists the title, the label and includes a brief critical annotation. Each recording is rated with a star system. The index lists all album titles.

356.   Harris, Steve. **Jazz on Compact Disc: A Critical Guide to the Best Recordings**. New York: Harmony/Crown, 1987. 176p. LCCN 87-7383. ISBN 0-517-56688-5. ML156.4.J3H31

A guide to "essential" jazz recordings. Brief biographical sketches are included for each of the 79 artists covered. Under each artist is listed selected CD recordings along with song titles, duration, date, label and number. Each recording is given a rating of one to three stars for performance and recording quality. [R: ARBA 1989, p. 491]

357.   Harrison, Max, Charles Fox and Eric Thacker. **The Essential**

Jazz Records: Volume 1, Ragtime to Swing. London: Mansell, 1984. Reprinted by Da Capo, 1988. LCCN 84-7926. ISBN 0-306-80326-7. ML156.4.J3H33

A selective collection of about 250 reviews of jazz LPs. The entries represent what the authors feel are the best recordings through the 1940s. Entries are divided into seven broad areas (the twenties, jazz in Europe, etc.) and include title, personnel, label, date and catalog number. [R: ARBA 1986, pp. 493-4; Choice, Mar 85, p. 966; RBB, Aug 85, p. 1647; WLB, Mar 85, p, 501]

358. Harrison, Max, et al. **Modern Jazz: The Essential Records**. London: Aquarius Books, 1978. 131p. LCCN 76-353404. ISBN 0-904619-01-X. ML156.4.J3M6

A selective compilation of over 200 reviews of jazz LPs recorded between 1945 and 1970. Entries are listed alphabetically by artist and include title, personnel, label and catalog number. [R: Notes, Sept 76, pp. 73-4 (an earlier printing)]

359. **Jazz on LP's: A Collectors' Guide to Jazz**. London: Decca Record Company Ltd., 1955. 282p. Reprinted by Greenwood Press, 1978. LCCN 78-3634. ISBN 0-313-20369-5. ML156.4.J3J44

A classic discography compiled for the jazz record collector. It is an annotated list of the complete jazz catalogs (as of 1955) of major jazz record labels. The labels covered are: Decca, Brunswick, London, Felsted, Ducretet-Thomson, Vogue Coral, Telefunken, and Durium. It is arranged alphabetically by artist/ensemble with some cross-references. Each entry includes a list of personnel and a brief biographical sketch.

360. Jones, Morley. **The Simon & Schuster Listener's Guide to Jazz**. Edited by Alan Rich. New York: Simon & Schuster, 1980. 133p. LCCN 80-5078. ISBN 0-671-25444-8. ML3506.R5

A selective discography of 50 prominent jazz artists. Each artist entry includes a brief biography and a selected and annotated discography.

361. Kernfeld, Barry, ed. **The Blackwell Guide to Recorded**

Jazz. Cambridge, MA: Basil Blackwell, 1991. 474p. LCCN 90-27658. ISBN 0-631-17164-9. ML156.4.J3B66

A selective guide to jazz recordings. It is arranged chronologically in 11 chapters. Each chapter begins with an historical overview of the style or era. One album is recommended for each important artist selected. About 125 recordings are covered. Each entry includes title, available formats (LP, cassette, CD), song titles, and personnel. There is a general index of song titles and personnel. [R: ARBA 1992, p. 534; RBB, Jan 15 1992, p. 966]

362.   Kingsbury, Paul, ed. **Country on Compact Disc: The Essential Guide to the Music**. New York: Grove Press, 1993.   286p.   LCCN   93-11887.   ISBN   0-8021-3379-7. ML156.4.C7C68

A guide to over 2,000 CD recordings by more than 500 country music artists. It is arranged alphabetically by artist, each includes a critical artist profile and a selected list of recordings. Each entry includes title, label, catalog number, and the year it was first issued. Each recording listed is given a rating of one to five stars. It also includes an alphabetically arranged list of number one country singles (based on Billboard Magazine charts), each listing the year it reached #1, the artist, and (when available) the CDs it can be found on. [R: Choice, June 1994, p. 1590]

363.   Lyons, Len. **The 101 Best Jazz Albums**. New York: William Morrow, 1980. 476p. LCCN 80-20735. ISBN 0-688-03720-8. ML3508.L93

Not only a buying guide but a history of jazz through available recordings. It is divided into the areas: ragtime; New Orleans; swing; bebop and early modern; modern (later styles); fusion; and free jazz. It includes a directory of record companies cited, and an index. [R: BL, Dec 1 1980, p. 496; LJ, Nov 15 1980, p. 2415; RSR, Apr 1981, p. 35]

364.   Marsh, Dave. **The Heart of Rock & Soul: The 1001 Greatest Singles Ever Made**. Ontario: New American Library, 1989. 717p. ISBN 0-452-26305-0. ML156.4.R6M37

An "opinionated guide" (back cover) to rock era singles. Songs are listed numerically (from number 1 - the best). Each entry includes composer(s), producer(s), label and number, year of release, and peak Billboard chart position. Each entry also includes a brief, informative, annotation (usually about a half page - but up to three pages long). The index includes both artists and song titles.

365.   McCartney, Albert et al. **Jazz on Record: A Critical Guide to the First 50 Years, 1917-1967**. New York: Oak, 1968. 416p. LCCN 68-57794. ISBN 0-8256-0111-8. ML156.4.J3J45

A broad (though selective), alphabetically arranged, list of jazz artist with brief biographies and significant discographies. It also contains brief essays that bring together artists under styles or idioms (e.g. Ragtime, Southern Blues, etc.). [R: Notes, June 70, pp. 556-8]

366.   Morethland, John. **The Best of Country Music**. Garden City, NY: Dolphin, 1984. 434p. LCCN 83-14238. ISBN 0-385-19192-8. ML156.4.C7M67

A collection of 100 full reviews, plus 650 brief commentaries, of what the author describes as the best country albums. Entries are divided by style/idioms and cross-referenced in the artist index.

367.   Oliver, Paul, ed. **The Blackwell Guide to Recorded Blues**. Rev. ed. Cambridge, MA: Basil Blackwell, 1989. 372p. LCCN 89-17734. ISBN 0-631-18301-9. ML156.4.B6B6

A critical guide to recorded blues music. It is divided into 12 areas or blues styles, each written by a British or American expert in that area. Each section includes a brief historical commentary and lists 10 "essential" recordings, as well as 30 additional recommended recordings. Entries include label and issue numbers, song titles, and a brief annotation. It includes a list of included LPs that were reissued on CD. It also includes a name index. [R: ARBA 1991, p. 531]

368.   Pruter, Robert, ed. **The Blackwell Guide to Soul Recordings**. Cambridge, MA: Blackwell, 1993. 496p. LCCN 93-12312. ISBN 0-631-18595-X. ML156.4.B6W55

A critical guide to soul recordings, mostly from the 1950s and

1960s. It is divided into ten sections beginning with Rhythm & Blues (the earliest recordings covered) and ending with Funk and Later Trends (the latest recordings covered. The eight remaining sections cover geographic areas (Detroit, Southwest, etc.). Each section begins with an historical overview, spot-lights ten essential recordings and lists up to 30 additional recommended recordings. The commentary tends to be more historical than critical. [R: choice, Mar 1994, p. 1088; Notes, Mar 95, pp. 959-61]

369.   Ramsey, Frederic, Jr. **A Guide to Longplay Jazz Records**. New York: Long Plater, 1954. Reprinted by Da Capo, 1977 (with new introduction by the author and supplementary listings). 282p. LCCN 77-9065. ISBN 0-306-70891-4. ML156.4.J3R3

A concise selective guide to jazz LPs issued through 1954. Entries are listed alphabetically by artist/ensemble and include: the album title; label and catalog number; song titles; and a brief annotation. There is an artist index and a song title index. [R: ARBA 1980, p. 442]

370.   Raymond, Jack. **Show Music on Record: The First One Hundred Years**. Rev. ed. Washington, DC: Smithsonian, 1992. 440p. LCCN 91-23483. ISBN 0-56098-151-2. ML156.4.O46R4

A comprehensive discography of original and studio cast albums. It covers from around 1890 through 1990. Entries are arranged by year of first performance and include composers, authors, librettists and performers. [R: ARBA 1984, p. 443 (1982 edition)]

371.   Robbins, Ira, ed. **The New Trouser Press Record Guide**. 4th ed. New York: Macmillan, 1991. 800p. ISBN 0-02-036361-3. ML156.4.P6N48

A collection of brief critical reviews of over 1,600 recordings. The focus is on independent labels and foreign releases. Entries are arranged alphabetically by artist/ensemble and include album titles, labels, and release dates. [R: RBB, Feb 1 1992, pp. 1053-4]

372.   Schleman, Hilton R. **Rhythm on Record**. Westport, CT:

Greenwood Press, 1978. Reprint of the 1936 edition. LCCN 77-28303. ISBN 0-313-20257-5. ML156.4.P6S34

"A complete survey and register of all the principal recorded dance music from 1906 to 1936, and a who's who of the artists concerned in the making" [from title page]. This is a discography of early dance music arranged alphabetically by artist or group. Each artist entry includes a brief biography and a list of recordings that includes song titles, record labels, catalog numbers, and year of recording. The personnel of groups are listed when the information is available. It includes an artist index (that includes all sidemen listed).

373. Scott, Frank & Down Home Music Staff. **The Down Home Guide to the Blues**. Chicago: A Capella Books, 1991. 250p. LCCN 90-37638. ISBN 0-55652-130-8. ML156.4.B6S26

A collection of over 3,000 reviews of all available blues recordings. It is arranged alphabetically by artist and includes country and urban blues, Cajun and zydeco, early jazz, boogie woogie, R&B and early rock. One hundred "most essential" blues records are flagged throughout the book. [R: ARBA 1992, pp. 530-1; RBB, Nov 1 1991, p. 562]

374. Scott, Frank and Al Ennis. **The Roots and Rhythm Guide to Rock**. Pennington, NJ: A Cappella Books, c1993. 383p. LCCN 93-8143. ISBN 1-55652-154-5. ML156.4.R6S3

A guide to rock and roll, rhythm and blues, rockabilly and doo wop recordings of the 1950s and 1960s. All recordings (about 4,000 in total) were in-print when the book was compiled. It is alphabetically arranged by artists/groups. Each entry includes a brief biography with album title(s) and label information. Some song selections are included for most recordings, and each record entry is coded to indicate album, cassette, and CD availability. It also includes a list of compilation albums, divided into two sections - rock and r&b/doo wop. Compilations are listed alphabetically by album title.

375. Shapiro, Bill. **Rock & Roll Review: A Guide to Good Rock on CD**. Kansas City, MO: Andrews and McMeel, 1991. 299p. ISBN 0-8362-6217-4. ML156.4.R6P7

A critical guide to more than 1,000 rock music CDs including reissues from the 1950s, as well as music issued on CDs through the 1980s. Inclusion is based solely upon the authors taste without consideration of record sales or artists' popularity. Entries are listed alphabetically by artist/group. The selected recordings include title, release date, label, issue number, running time, rating (A to F) and critical annotation. Brief background notes are included for most artists.

376.   Swenson, John, ed. **The Rolling Stone Jazz Record Guide**. New York: Rolling Stone/Random House, 1985. 219p. LCCN 84-42510. ISBN 0-394-72643-X. ML156.4.J3S9

A critical guide to over 4,000 jazz LPs. It is limited to recordings commercially available at the time of writing. It is arranged by artist. Each entry includes a brief commentary and a list of recordings with label and a one to five star rating. [R: ARBA 1986, p. 494; BL, July 85, p. 1500]

377.   Tobler, John. **100 Great Albums of the Sixties**. Woodstock, NY: Overlook Press, 1994. LCCN 94-25581. ISBN 0-879515-69-4. ML156.4.P6T63

A chronologically arranged list of the best LPs released through the 1960s. Nearly half of the entries were releases in 1968 and 1969. Each entry includes the album title, artists, song titles, producers, total running time, label, and jacket photo.

378.   Tudor, Dean and Nancy Tudor. **Black Music**. (American Popular Music on Elpee.) Littleton, CO: Libraries Unlimited, 1979. 262p. LCCN 78-15563. ISBN 0-87287-147-9. ML156.4.P6T8

From the three volume series of selective discographies of American popular music idioms, it is intended as both a survey and a buying guide to commercial recordings of Black music idioms. It is divided into the broad categories: (1) blues; (2) rhythm 'n' blues; (3) Gospel; (4) soul; and (5) Reggae. Approximately 1,300 recordings are listed, with about 220 identified as "core" purchases. Entries include album title, record label and catalog number; followed by a brief critical annotation. The most important discs, selected by the authors, are starred (*). It includes a directory of record company addresses followed by the titles and catalog numbers of their "starred" releases. It also includes an artist index. [R:

ARBA 1980, p. 443; WLB, May 79, p. 656 (Black Music)]

379. Tudor, Dean and Nancy Tudor. **Contemporary Popular Music**. (American Popular Music on Elpee.) Littleton, CO: Libraries Unlimited, 1979. 313p. LCCN 78-32124. ISBN 0-87287-191-6. ML156.4.P6T83

A critical guide to mostly American popular music recorded on long-playing discs and tapes. It is divided into two general areas: mainstream popular music (including big bands, dance bands, stage music, film music, and vocal song stylists), and rock music (divided into styles including: rockabilly, blues rock country/folk rock, and heavy metal). More than 700 albums are listed with more than 200 identified as seminal recordings. Each entry includes the artist, label, number, and brief descriptive and critical annotation. Anthologies are included in most categories. It includes artist indexes for both sections. [R: ARBA 1980, p. 443; WLB, Oct 79, p. 130]

380. Tudor, Dean and Nancy Tudor. **Grass Roots Music**. Littleton, CO: Libraries Unlimited, 1979. 367p. LCCN 78-31686. ISBN 0-87287-133-9. ML156.4.N3U7

A buying guide to LP recordings of country music, bluegrass, old-time music, American and British folk music, troubadour, and sacred music. About 1,700 discs are listed with annotations, while about 200 are identified as "first purchase." Entries are listed under genre. It includes an artist index. [R: ARBA 1981, pp. 443-4]

381. Tudor, Dean and Nancy Tudor. **Jazz**. Littleton, CO: Libraries Unlimited, 1979. (American Popular Music on Elpee.) 302p. ML156.4.J3T73

A selective list of jazz recordings on LPs. It is divided into the broad categories: (1) ragtime; (2) geographic origins and stylings; (3) mainstream swing and big bands; (4) bop, cool, modern; and (5) diverse themes. The categories are then further subdivided with approximately 1,300 recordings listed. Entries include album title, record label and catalog number; followed by a brief critical annotation. It contains an artist index. [R: ARBA 1980, p. 444; Choice, July 1979, p. 651; LJ, Apr 15 1979, p. 940; Notes, Mar 1980, p. 648; RSR, Apr 1981, p. 32; WLB, May 1979, p. 655]

382. Tudor, Dean. **Popular Music: An Annotated Guide to Recordings**. Littleton, CO: Libraries Unlimited, 1983. 647p. LCCN 83-18749. ISBN 0-87287-395-1. ML156.4.P6T85

An update of the four 1979 titles: Jazz, Black Music, Grass Roots Music, and Contemporary Popular Music. This is critical survey of recorded American popular music. It is divided into the broad genre headings: Black music, folk music, jazz music, mainstream music, popular religious music, and rock music. These headings are divided into narrower musical styles. More than 6,000 recordings are listed. Entries include album titles, labels, catalog numbers, and brief annotations. It includes an artist index. [R: ARBA 1985, pp. 438-9; BL, Apr 15 1984, p. 1149; LJ, May 1 1984, p. 890; RBB, Dec 1 1984, p. 508; WLB, June 84, pp. 753-4]

383. Wynn, Ron, Michael Erlewine and Vladimir Bogdanov. **The All Music Guide to Jazz: The Best CDs, Albums & Tapes**. San Francisco: Miller Freeman, 1994. 751p. LCCN 94-11273. ISBN 0-87930-308-5. ML156.4.J3A45

A collection of more than 1,100 profiles of recorded jazz artists each with a selected list of recordings (CDs, albums and cassettes). Most recordings are briefly reviewed and rated. It also includes brief profiles of jazz record producers, record labels, and jazz clubs/venues. There are glossaries of jazz terms and styles and an artist index.

Guidebooks

384. Bird, Christiane. **The Jazz and Blues Lover's Guide to the U.S.** Reading, MA: Addison Wesley, 1991. LCCN 90-46545. ISBN 0-201-52332-9. ML3508.B57

A guide, by U.S. city, to night clubs and restaurants that feature live jazz and blues music. A brief history of jazz and blues for each city is included. Local publications, that give day-to-day listings for these establishments, are also listed. [R: ARBA 1992, p. 534; LJ, Mar 15, 1991, p. 83]

385. Fein, Art. **The L.A. Musical History Tour: A Guide to the Rock and Roll Landmarks of Los Angeles**. Winchester, MA: Faber and Faber, 1990. 139p. LCCN 90-3427. ISBN 0-517-12932-3. ML3534 .F45

A collection of brief descriptions of over 200 music related sights throughout Los Angeles. These include famous recording studios, clubs, stores, album cover sites, and grave sites.

386. Millard, Bob. **Music City USA: The Country Music Lover's Guide to Nashville and Tennessee**. 228p. New York: Harper Collins, c1993. LCCN 92-54686. ISBN 0-06-273229-3. ML3524.M54

A travel guide for the state of Tennessee designed for the country music fan. It primarily focuses on Nashville, but includes Memphis, Knoxville, Chattanooga, Pidgeon Falls and Gatlinburg. Though the focus is on country music attractions and venues, other avenues of family entertainment are explored. Hotel and dining recommendations are included.

387.   Nolan, A. M. **Rock 'N' Roll Road Trip : The Ultimate Guide to the Sites, the Shrines, and the Legends across America**. New York: Pharos Books, 1992. 229p. LCCN 92-20229. ISBN 0-088687-700-8. ML3534.N64

A traveler's guide to sights that are significant to the history of rock music. It is divided into four geographic areas and focuses on sixteen cities and their surrounding areas. Under each city is listed the clubs, studios, record stores, and any other historically significant location.

388.   Walker, Dave. **American Rock N' Roll Tour**. New York: Thunder Mouth Press, 1992. 260p. ISBN 0-56025-041-0. ML3534.W28

A guide to U.S. rock music landmarks. It lists clubs, concert halls, museums, and historical sights. It is divided into five broad geographic areas. States and cities are listed alphabetically with sights described in full. The index includes the names of the sites, as well as the artists connected with them.

389.   Weil, Susanne and Barry Singer. **Steppin' Out: A Guide to Live Music in Manhattan**. Charlotte, NC: East Wood Press, 1980. LCCN 79-23812. ISBN 0-914788-24-8. ML15.N3W4

A critical guidebook to 150 New York night spots that feature live music. Each chapter is devoted to a musical style (jazz, cabaret, etc.).

390.   Wooton, Richard. **Honky Tonkin': A Travel Guide to American Music**. Charlotte, NC: East Wood Press, 1980. LCCN 80-508. ISBN 0-914788-26-4. ML19.W66

A critical guidebook by city (or sometimes state) of night clubs and the style of music each specializes in. The styles are limited to rock music and styles that impact rock music. It also includes lists of record stores, radio stations, and festivals. [R: ARBA 1982, p. 510]

Almanacs and Chronologies

391.   Aquila, Richard. **That Old Time Rock & Roll: A Chronicle of an Era, 1954-1963.** New York: Schirmer Books, 1989. 370p.   LCCN 89-2384.   ISBN 0-02-870081-3; 0-02-870082-1 (pbk.) ML3534.A68

An almanac covering the first decade of the rock era. It begins with an historical overview plus a year-by-year listing of important news items, sports facts, life styles (trivia), and the top movies, TV shows and hit records (very selective). The second section (the largest) consists of over 80 lists and sublists of song titles divided by themes and topics (cars, school, alcohol, movies, politics, musical styles, etc.). This section also contains a list of the top forty songs for each year covered. The third section is an alphabetical list of artists and ensembles with brief career annotations. [R: ARBA 1990, p.545]

392.   Biracree, Tim. **The Country Music Almanac.** Englewood Cliffs, NJ: Prentice Hall, 1993. 288p. LCCN 93-9355. ISBN 0-671-7976-1. ML3524.B57

A collection of general information on Country music. It is divided into three major sections: the country tradition (includes a chronology of important events in country music and the biographies of the persons in the Country Music Hall of Fame), who's who... (includes biographies of 23 prominent Country artists), country songs (includes a list of all certified gold and platinum songs - arranged by artist). It also includes lists of country music award winners and a general index.

393.   Bordman,   Gerald.   **American   Musical   Theatre: A
       Chronicle**. 2d ed. New York: Oxford, 1992. 821 p. LCCN 91-
       15671. ISBN 0-19-507242-1. ML1711.B67

       A year-by-year history of the musical theater. It is divided
       into 12 sections, starting with 1866 (the origins) through 1990.
       It is written in a commentary style with show titles in bold
       letters. It includes an index of show titles, an index of song
       titles, and an index of persons. [R: Notes, Mar 1994, pp. 985-
       88]

394.   Cotten, Lee.   **Shake Rattle & Roll: The Golden Age of
       American Rock & Roll, Volume I 1952-1955**. Ann Arbor:
       Pierian Press, 1989. LCCN 87-63455. ISBN 0-87650-246-X.
       ML3534.C69

       A chronology of rock music industry events. Each year begins
       with brief history. Each month ends with a top ten list and an
       "artist of the month" biography. It includes a performer index,
       a song index, a record company index, an industry personnel
       index, a broadcast media index, and a bibliography. [R: ARBA
       1990, pp. 546-7; Choice, Sept 89, p. 76; LJ, Sept 15, 1989, p.
       104; WLB, June 89, p. 127]

395.   Green, Stanley.   **Hollywood Musicals Year by Year**.
       Milwaukee, WI: Hal Leonard Pub. Corp., c1990. 372p. ISBN
       0-88188-836-2. PN1995.9.M86 G74

       A selective guide to more than 300 on and off Broadway
       musical shows from 1866 to 1989. Entries are arranged under
       the date that the show opened and include: composers,
       authors, producers, directors, choreographers, cast, song titles,
       length of New York run, the New York theatre where it
       opened, and a brief commentary about the production and
       plot. It includes a show title index, a composer/lyricist index,
       a librettist index, a director index, a choreographer index, a
       major cast member index, and a theatre index.

396.   Hendler, Herb. **Year by Year in the Rock Era**. Westport,
       CT: Greenwood Press, 1983. 350p. LCCN 82-11722. ISBN 0-
       313-23456-6. ML3534.H45

       Arranged by year (1954 to 1981), it is not so much about rock
       music, but rather "the history sociology and economics that

influenced and were influenced by the rock generations."
(Preface) Each year is divided by: artists; selected recordings;
dances; rock news; news that influenced rock; statistics;
teen/college life styles; fashion; fads; slang; the new woman in
rock; and trivia. This is followed by lists and tables including:
costs and tuition's, TV, movies, magazines, etc. It includes a
bibliography but no index. [R: ARBA 1985, pp. 440-1; Choice,
Oct 84, p. 248; RBB, Dec 1 1984, p. 514; WLB, May 84, P.
678]

397.   Lauferberg, Frank. **Rock and Pop, Day by Day**. London:
       Blandford Press (New York: Sterling), 1992. 391p. ISBN 0-
       7173-2319-X

       A collection of birthdates, deathdates and important pop music
       related facts arranged by date (January 1 through December
       31). It includes song titles of single recordings that reached
       number one on each day of the year. It includes an index of
       names and an index of group names.

398.   Marsh, Dave and Kevin Stein. **The Book of Rock Lists**.
       New York: Dell Publishing Co., c1981. LCCN 81-9778. ISBN
       0-440-57580-X. ML3534.M37

       Divided into 34 chapters, each representing a very broad
       subject, the authors have collected hundreds of comparative
       lists. Most are "best of..." (20 best harmonica players, 10 best
       rock TV shows), "worst of..." (10 worst debut singles, worst
       teeth), or simply interesting/odd groupings (artists who made
       commercials, Biblical characters in Bob Dylan's lyrics).

399.   Millard, Bob. **Country Music: 70 Years of America's
       Favorite Music**. New York: Harper Collins, 1993. 416p.
       LCCN 92-56276. ISBN 0-06-273244-7. ML3524. M53

       Arranged by year (1920 through 1992), each year includes
       industry milestones (important events), important recordings,
       debut artists, and artist profiles. It also lists Country Music
       Association Awards, Academy of Country Music Awards, as
       well as Country music Grammys and Gold/Platinum Awards.
       It includes a name index and an index of song titles. [R: LJ,
       Nov 15 1993, p. 72]

400. **1993 "This Day In Music" Almanac.**   Boston: BPI
      Entertainment News Wire, 1993.

      Divided by day of the year (January 1, 1993 to December 31,
      1993), this is a listing of significant popular music news items.
      It is primarily a tool for radio programmers, with items listed
      under each date in order by year (the most current first). Data
      is from BPI-owned publication including Billboard Magazine
      and the focus is on rock era information. Artists birthdates
      are also listed citing both year and place.

401. Nite, Norm N.   **Rock On Almanac: The First Four**
      Decades of Rock 'n' Roll, a chronology.   New York:
      Harper & Row, 1989. 533p.   LCCN 89-54109.   ISBN 0-06-
      055166-6. ML3534.N58

      Intended to "show chronologically the history, events, music
      and people that helped shape rock 'n' roll" (introduction). It is
      arranged by year, covering from 1954 to 1989. Each chapter
      includes: general news highlights; sports winners; music high-
      lights; debut artists with their debut singles; other artists
      (name only); hit singles by month; top singles of the year (10);
      top albums of the year (10); Grammy winners (major awards);
      births and deaths; selected movies; selected academy award
      winners; and top television shows. It includes a glossary of
      terms, an artist index and a song title index.

402. **Rolling Stone Rock Almanac: The Chronicles of Rock &**
      Roll. New York: Macmillan, 1983. LCCN 83-16178. ISBN 0-
      02-604490-0. ML102.R6R66

      A day-by-day chronology of rock music from January 1954 to
      December 1982.   Each year begins with an overview.   It
      includes charts of the number one recordings for each week
      covered. Indexed. [R: ARBA 1985, pp. 441-2]

403. Tobler, John. **This Day in Rock: Day by Day Record of**
      Rock's Biggest News Stories. New York: Carroll & Graf,
      1993. LCCN 93-24665. ISBN 0-8818-4860-3. ML3534.T64

      A compilation of birth dates, death dates and important news
      items related to rock music. All are arranged by day of the
      year.

404.   Whitburn, Joel. **Joel Whitburn Presents Daily #1 Hits: A
       Day by Day Listing of the #1 Pop Records of the Past 50
       Years, 1940-1989**. Menomonee Falls, WI: Record Research,
       Inc., c1989.   378p.   LCCN 90-143818.   ISBN 0-89820-095-4.
       ML156.4.P6W4575

       Arranged by calendar year, from January 1 to December 31,
       one page for each day of the year. Under each year is listed all
       of the number one songs from 1940 into 1993. Each song entry
       includes title, artist and number of days it remained at
       number one. It includes a title index. [R: ARBA 1994, p. 559]

Yearbooks

405. Feather, Leonard. **The Encyclopedic Yearbook of Jazz**. New York: Horizon, 1956. Reprinted by Da Capo 1991. LCCN 89-26063. ISBN 0-306-76289-7

A compilation of articles, by the author and others, on current events and trends in jazz. It also includes biographies that update and expand The Encyclopedia of Jazz (Feather, 1955).

406. Feather, Leonard. **The New Yearbook of Jazz**. New York: Horizon, 1958. Reprinted by Da Capo 1985. LCCN 55-10778. ISBN 0-306-76288-9

Volume three in a series that included The Encyclopedia of Jazz (Feather, 1955. Not listed) and The Encyclopedic Yearbook of Jazz (Feather, 1956). It updates and expands previous volumes.

407. Whitburn, Joel, comp. **Billboard 1991 Music and Video Yearbook**. Menomonee Falls, WI: Record Research, 1992. 288p. annual. ISBN 0-89820-081-4

A compilation of Billboard Magazine's record and video charts for 1991. It is intended as an update to all Whitburn/Billboard discographies. It is divided into three parts: the singles, the albums, and the videos. First is a list of all Hot 100 songs by peak position (All number one songs, followed by all number two songs, etc.). Each entry lists the performer, the date peaked, and the playing time. This is followed by compilations of the singles charts (Hot 100, Country, R&B, Adult Contemporary), the Album Rock Tracks chart and the Modern Rock Tracks chart; each arranged alphabetically by artist. Entries from each of these charts include song title, label & number, debut date, peak chart position, and number of weeks charted. This is followed by an index of all song titles listed.

The album section includes compilations of the Top Albums, Country Albums, and R&B Albums charts. Each compilation is arranged alphabetically by artist and includes album title, label & number, debut date, peak chart position, and number of weeks charted. These are followed by lists of the number one albums from the remainder of the album charts (Latin, Classical, Jazz, New Age, etc.) and the international charts.

The video section begins with an alphabetical, annotated, list of videos that debuted on the Top Video Rental and Top Video Sales charts. Each entry lists peak chart positions and dates; publisher and catalog numbers; playing time; director; producer(s); stars; and description. This is followed by lists of the number one videos from all of the video charts (Top Rentals, Top Sales, Top Videodisc Sales, Top Music Videos, Top Kid Video, and Top Special Interest Videos). [R: ARBA 1992, p. 528 (1990 issue)]

Miscellaneous

408. Appice, Carmine. **Carmine Appice Presents the Drum Superstars.** Secaucus, NJ: Warner Brothers, 1990. 80p.

A collection of reprints from the author's Drum Beat column from Circus magazine. More than 60 drummers are included. The entries are analytical (rather than biographical), featuring the authors insights into the playing techniques of the artists covered. Each entry includes musical examples.

409. Avedis Zildjian Co. **Cymbal Set-Ups of Famous Drummers**. Accord MA: Avedis Zildjian Co., [?].

A promotional publication of the cymbal manufacturer. It diagrams the cymbal placement in the trap-sets of fifty-two drummers.

410. Ballou, Glen, ed. **Handbook for Sound Engineers: The New Audio Cyclopedia**. Indianapolis, IN: Howard W Sams & Co., 1987. 1,247p. LCCN 85-50023. ISBN 0-672-21983-2. TK7881.4.H361

It is intended to be the definitive reference source for sound engineers. It is divided into seven broad subject areas: acoustics; electronic components; electroacoustic devices; circuits and equipment; recording and playback; design applications; and measurements. All subjects begin with very basic information, then develop more details. This allows the book to be effective at all levels of understanding. It includes a general index.

411.   Clayton, Peter and Peter Gammond. **The Guinness Jazz A-Z.** London: Guinness, 1986.   262p.   ISBN 0-8160-2564-9. ML102.J2

Not a "who's who" but a "what's what" of jazz.   It includes musical terms, slang, significant geographic locations, jazz clubs, nicknames, dances, instruments, etc.   [R: ARBA 1988, p. 524]

412.   Chu, John and Elliot Cafritz. **The Music Video Guide.** New York: McGraw-Hill, 1986. 412p. LCCN 85-7918. ISBN 0-07-010865-X. PN1992.8.M87C46

A guide to 500 home music video titles, including performance, concert and soundtrack titles.   Entries include title, artist or cast, running time, distributor, and price.   Entries are arranged alphabetically under each division: rock videos, rock concert videos, rock musicals, movie musicals, pop/adult, Black artists, country/folk, jazz, family entertainment, and performing arts.   Annotations are critical, include background information on the artist(s), and usually list song titles.   [R: ARBA 1987, p. 484; BL, Mar 15, 1986, p. 1052; Choice, June 86, p. 1518]

413.   Dolgins, Adam.   **Rock Names**. New York: Citadel Press, 1993.   237p.   LCCN 92-32216.   ISBN 0-8065-1363-2. ML102.R6D66

An alphabetical list of rock group names and pseudonyms of individuals with brief explanation of their origins. (e.g. The group ABBA derived their name from the first initials of each of the four members.)

414.   Franks, Don.   **Tony, Grammy, Emmy, Country: A Broadway, Television and Records Awards Reference**. Jefferson, NC: McFarland, 1986. 202p. ISBN 0-89950-204-0. PN2270.A93F7

A complete list of Tony awards (1947 through 1984); Emmy Awards (1948 through 1984); Grammy Awards (1959 through 1984); and Country Music Association Awards (1967 through 1984). The index lists all recipients.

415.   Ganzl, Kurt and Andrew Lamb. **Ganzl's Book of the Musical Theatre.** New York: Schirmer Books, 1989. 1353p. ISBN 0-02-871941-7

A guide to more than 300 selected musicals. The authors include German, French and Spanish productions with the expected American and British entries. Each entry includes a plot summary with song settings as well as a complete list of song titles. It includes a general index.

416.   Green, Jonathan, comp. **The Book of Rock Quotes**. New York: Delilah/Putnam, c1982. 128p. ISBN 0-399-41000-7

A collection of brief quotes by rock musicians. Entries were gathered from books, magazines, radio and TV shows, and record sleeves. Each entry lists the artist's name but not the source. It is divided into 20 broad subject areas.

417.   Krenshaw, Marshall. **Hollywood Rock: A Guide to Rock 'n' Roll in the Movies**. New York: HarperCollins, c1994. 351p. ISBN 0-06-273242-0

A listing of more than 300 movies about rock, rock movie musicals, movies with rock stars as actors, movies with influential rock soundtracks, and full-length rock documentaries. Films are listed alphabetically by title. Each entry includes director, producer, cast, screenwriter, studio, length, a qualitative (star) rating, and a brief profile of the film. It includes a name index.

418.   Lynch, Richard Chigley. **Musicals: A Complete Selection Guide. For Local Productions**. Chicago: American Library Association, 1993. LCCN 93-27387. ISBN 0-838-90627-3. ML19.L9

A directory of nearly 400 musicals aimed at the amateur production company. Each entry includes title, writers, date of first production, publisher (music, as well as libretto), licensing agent and cast size. Each also include a brief description from a production stand-point. The two appendixes are directories of licensing agents and music publishers. It is indexed by composer, lyricist and librettist.

419. Lucha-Burns, Carol. **Musical Notes: A Practical Guide to Staffing and Staging Standards of the American Musical Theatre**. New York: Greenwood Press, 1986. LCCN 85-10017. ISBN 0-313-24648-3. MT955.L8

An alphabetical list of musical theatre titles with background, history, synopsis, songs of special interest (annotated), instrumentation and publisher. It includes three ndexes: shows and years of production, songs and their sources, professionals and their specialties.

420. McGee, Mark Thomas. **The Rock and Roll Movie Encyclopedia of the 1950s**. Jefferson, NC: McFarland, 1990. 224p. LCCN 89-43657. ISBN 0-89950-500-7. PN1995.9.M86M4

A guide to selected 1950s movies that contain performances (some live, some lip-synched) by rock musicians. Entries are listed by movie title and include plot summaries, production notes, historical background, and details of the musical performances. Each entry also lists the cast, release date, production credits and quotes from the movie's reviews. There are two appendices: one lists song titles and the films they are from, the other lists performers and the song titles they sang on film. The index lists names and song titles.

421. Meeker, David. **Jazz in the Movies: A Guide to Jazz Musicians 1917-1977**. Rev. ed. New Rochelle, New York: Da Capo, 1982. 336p. LCCN 77-30238. ISBN 0-306-76147-5. ML128.M7M38

An annotated, alphabetical list of over 2,500 films in which jazz musicians either appear on screen or contribute to the soundtrack. It includes Soundies and Sander Telescriptions. It is indexed by artist. [R: ARBA 1978, p. 469; BL, May 15 1978, p. 1519-20; Notes, Mar 79, p. 636 (1st ed.)]

422. O'Neil, Thomas. **The Grammys: For the Record**. New York: Penguin, 1993. 598p. ISBN 0-1401-6651-2

A listing of all Grammy nominees and winners from 1958 (the first awards) through 1991. Each year includes a commentary about the nominated music, nominated artists, and the awards ceremony. It includes an index of names and titles.

423.   Sandahl, Linda J. **Rock Films: A Viewer's Guide to Three Decades of Musicals, Concerts, Documentaries, and Soundtracks, 1955-1986**. New York: Facts On File, 1987. 239p. LCCN 86-24347. ISBN 0-8160-1281-4; 0-8160-1576-7 (pbk.). PN1995.9.M86S26

A listing of rock feature films, divided in three sections: musicals; concerts and documentaries; and soundtracks. It includes an index of film titles, an index of names (artists or groups), and an index of song titles. [R: ARBA 1988, p. 526; BL, May 1 1987, p. 1328; RQ, Sum 87, p. 520]

424.   Sutton, Allan, comp. **A Guide to Pseudonyms on American Records, 1892-1942**. Westport, CT: Greenwood Press, 1993. 149p. LCCN 93-4768. ISBN 0-313-29060-1. ML158.S9

A compilation of pseudonyms, used by artists and groups, on domestic and foreign issue recordings. It covers jazz, blues, gospel, country, mainstream popular and classical artists. Entries are listed alphabetically by pseudonym under three categories: (1) vocalists and vocal groups (2) domestic, vocalists and vocal groups, and (3) foreign, and instrumental soloists and groups. Entries generally indicate the record label on which the pseudonym is found. Entries for ensembles often list their membership. It contains two appendices: legal names (a list of professional names of artists with their actual names), and a list of record labels and affiliates. It includes two indexes, one for vocalists and vocal groups, the other for instrumental soloists and groups. Each lists artists by their professional names, cross-referenced to the pseudonyms they recorded under. [R: ARBA 1994, p. 540; Choice, Mar 1994, p. 1106]

425.   Taft, Michael. **Blues Lyric Poetry: A Concordance**. New York: Garland, 1983. 3 v. (Garland Reference Library of the Humanities, v. 362) LCCN 83-48630. ISBN 0-8240-9236-8. PS309.B55T33

An alphabetical, key word in context, thesaurus of the full lyrics to over 2,000 blues songs. The songs were recorded by more than 350 singers between 1920 and 1942. A discography of the songs and a word frequency list are included. [R: ARBA 1985, p. 439; Choice, Dec 84, p. 542]

426.   Terenzio, Maurice, Scott MacGillivray and Ted Okuda. **The Soundies Distributing Corporation of America: A History and Filmography of their "Jukebox" Musical Films of the 1940s**. Jefferson, NC: McFarland, 1991. 224p. LCCN 90-53527. ISBN 0-89950-578-3. PN1995.9.M86T47

This book begins with a brief history of the musical shorts produced in the 1940s. This is followed by a Filmography (the main body of the book) that lists all Soundies arranged by copyright date. Each entry includes title, date, producer, director, production firm, and cast (musicians & actors). The authors also include title lists of Vis-o-graph, Featurettes and Telescriptions products (all 'Soundies-like' musical shorts). These include artists' names when available. There is an index of Soundies titles, but no artist index.

427.   Warner, Alan. **Who Sang What on the Screen**. London: Angus and Robertson, 1984. ISBN 0-207-14869-4. ML128.R6W37

A source book of vocal music from, or related to, movies and television. Entries are divided into 12 subject areas, the largest being Movie Musical Songs. The areas are tied together by an index of song titles, an index of artists, and an index of movie titles and television program names.

Appendix A: Individual Discographies

These discographies are listed alphabetically by subject without annotations. When two or more discographies are combined into one volume, it is listed under each artist's name.

AC/DC

> Tesch, Chris. **AC/DC: An Illustrated Record Collector's Guide**. U.S.A.: C.M. Tesch, 1992. LCCN 92-208222. ML156.7.A25T5

Acuff, Roy

> Schlappi, Elizabeth. **Roy Acuff and his Smoky Mountain Boys: Discography**. Rev. and enl. Cheswold, DE: Disc Collector Publications, 1966. 36p. LC 88-112375. ML156.7.A3S3

Alexander, Van

> Garrod, Charles. **Al Donahue and his Orchestra. Van Alexander and his Orchestra**. Zephyrhills, FL: Joyce Record Club Publication, 1991. LCCN 93-167129.

Andrew Sisters

> Garrod, Charles. **The Andrew Sisters**. Zephyrhills, FL: Joyce Record Club Publication, 1992. LCCN 93-136872

Anthony, Ray

> Garrod, Charles. **Ray Anthony and his Orchestra**. Zephyrhills, FL: Joyce Record Club Publication, 1988. LC 88-202991. ML156.7.A57G4

Armstrong, Louis

Jepsen, Jorgen Grunnet. **A Discography of Louis Armstrong, 1923-1971**. Kobenhavn: Knudsen, 1973. LCCN 75-325974. ML156.7.A75J4

Westerberg, Hans. **Boy from New Orleans: Louis "Satchmo" Armstrong on Records, Films, Radio and Television**. Copenhagen: Jazzmedia, c1981. 220p. LCCN 82-112772. ML156.7.A75 W5

Auld, Georgie

Garrod, Charles and Bill Korst. **Georgie Auld and his Orchestra**. Zephyrhills, FL: Joyce Record Club Publication, 1992. LCCN 93-151529

Ayres, Mitchell

Garrod, Charles. **Mitchell Ayres and his Orchestra**. Zephyrhills, FL: Joyce Record Club Publication, 1991. 31p. LCCN 93-167096

Baez, Joan

Swanekamp, Joan. **Diamonds and Rust: a Bibliography and Discography on Joan Baez**. Ann Arbor, MI: Pieran Press, 1980.

Baker, Chet

Lerfeldt, Hans Henrik and Thorbjorn Sjogren. **Chet: The Discography of Chesney Henry Baker**. Copenhagen: JazzMedia, [1991].

Barnet, Charlie

Garrod, Charles. **Charlie Barnet and his Orchestra**. Rev. Zephyrhills, FL: Joyce Music Publication, 1984. LCCN 87-120873. ML156.7.B37 G4

Jazz Discographies Unlimited Presents Charlie Barnet and his Orchestra. Rev. ed. Whittier, CA: ErnGeoBil Publications, 1967. LCCN 82-222555. ML156.7.B37J4

Basie, Count

Garrod, Charles. **Count Basie and his Orchestra**.

Zephyrhills, FL: Joyce Record Club, 1987-1989. 3 v. LCCN 88-169740. ML156.7.B38G3

Sheridan, Chris. **Count Basie: a Bio-Discography**. Westport, CT: Greenwood Press, 1986. 1350p. LCCN 86-9916. ML156.7.B38S5

The Beatles

Castleman, Harry. **All Together Now: The First Complete Beatles Discography, 1961-1975.** Ann Arbor, MI: Pierian Press, 1976. 385p. LCCN 77-151852. ML156.7.B4C36

Castleman, Harry. **The End of the Beatles?** Ann Arbor, MI: Pierian Press, 1985. 553p. LCCN 84-60639. ML156.7.B4C38

Lewisohn, Mark. **The Beatles Recording Sessions**. New York: Harmony Books, 1990. 204p LCCN 90-194604. ML156.7.B4L5

McCoy, William. **Every Little Thing: The Definitive Guide to Beatles Recording Variations, Rare Mixes & Other Musical Oddities, 1958-1986**. Ann Arbor, MI: Popular Culture, Ink, 1990. 368 p. LCCN 89-92321. ML156.7.B4M3

Reinhart, Charles. **You Can't Do That: Beatles Bootlegs & Novelty Records**. Chicago: Contemporary Books, c1981. 431p. LC 84-12748. ML156.7.B4R4

Russell, J.P. **The Beatles Album File and Complete Discography**. Poole, Dorset: Blandford Press, 1982.

Schwartz, David. **Listening to the Beatles: An Audiophile's Guide to the Sound of the Fab Four**. Ann Arbor, MI: Popular Culture, Ink, 1990. LC 89-92316. ML156.7.B4S4

Stannard, Neville. **The Long and Winding Road: A History of the Beatles on Record.** 2nd ed. New York: Avon, 1984. 240p. LCCN 83-45915. ML156.7.B4S7

Wallgren, Mark. **The Beatles on Record.** New York: Simon & Schuster, c1982. 336p. LCCN 82-10305. ML156.7.B4W3

Wiener, Allen J. **The Beatles: A Recording History**. Jefferson, NC: McFarland, c1986. 614p. LCCN 85-43597. ML156.7.B4W5

Wiener, Allen J. **The Beatles: The Ultimate Recording**

Guide. New York: Facts on File, c1992. 291p. LCCN 91-40635 ISBN 0-8160-2511-8. ML156.7.B4W53

Wlaschek, Mathias. **The Beatles, Here, There (and Everywhere?)**. Koln: Modern Music Cologne, c1983. 416p. LCCN 86-137274. ML156.7.B4W6

Bechet, Sidney

Mauerer, Hans J. **A Discography of Sidney Bechet**. Copenhagen: Karl Emil Knudsen, 1969. 83p. LCCN 4-554374. ML156.7.B42 M4

Beiderbecke, Bix

Castelli, Vittorio. **The Bix Bands: a Bix Beiderbecke Disco-Biography.** Milan: Raretone, 1972. 233p. LCCN 79-111637. ML156.7.B44C4

Beneke, Tex

Garrod, Charles. **Tex Beneke and his Orchestra**. Rev. Zephyrhills, FL: Joyce Music Studio, 1986. LCCN 87-121645. ML156.7.B46G4

Berigan, Bunny

Danca, Vince. **Bunny: A Bio-Discography of Jazz Trumpeter Bunny Berigan.** Rockford, IL: Danca, 1978.

Bernie, Ben

Garrod, Charles. **Ben Bernie and his Orchestra**. Zephyrhills FL: Joyce Record Club Publication, 1991. 19p. LCCN 92-195251. ML156.7.B466G3

Berry, Leon Chu

Evensmo, Jan. **The Tenor Saxophone of Leon Chu Berry, with a Critical Assessment of all his Known Records and Broadcasts**. Hosle, Norway: J. Evensmo, 1976. 36p. LCCN 82-210371. ML156.7.B47E9

Bothwell, Johnny

Garrod, Charles. **Boyd Raeburn and his Orchestra, Plus Johnny Bothwell and George Handy**. Zephyrhills, FL: Joyce Music, 1985. LCCN 87-121644. ML156.7.R33G3

Bowie, David

Fletcher, David Jeffrey. **David Robert Jones Bowie: The Discography of a Generalist, 1962-1979**. Chicago: F. Fergeson Productions, 1979.

Kamp, Thomas. **David Bowie, The Wild-Eyed Boy, 1964-1984: A Comprehensive Reference and World-Wide Discography Guide.** Phoenix, AZ: O'Sullivan Woodside (distributed by Caroline House), c1985. 184p.   LCCN 85-7158. ML156.7.B69K35

Bradley, Will

Garrod, Charles. **Will Bradley and his Orchestra; plus, Freddie Slack and his Orchestra**. Zephyrhills, FL: Joyce Music Publication, 1986. LCCN 87-119948. ML156.7.B72G4

Braxton, Anthony

Wachtmeister, Hans. **A Discography & Bibliography of Anthony Braxton**. Stocksund, Sweden: Blue Anchor, c1982. LCCN 86-228200. ML156.7.B738W2

Bridges, Henry

Evensmo, Jan. **The Tenor Saxophones of Henry Bridges, Robert Carroll, Herschal Evans, Johnny Russell: with a Critical Assessment of all their Known Records and Broadcasts.** Hosle, Norway: J. Evensmo, 1976. LCCN 82-210390. ML156.4.J3E93

Brooks, Randy

Garrod, Charles. **Bobby Sherwood and his Orchestra; Randy Brooks and his Orchestra.** Zephyrhills, FL: Joyce Record Club Publication, 1987. LCCN 88-173112. ML156.7.S5G4

Brown, Les

Garrod, Charles. **Les Brown and his Orchestra, 1936-1960**. Zephyrhills, FL: Joyce Record Club Publication, 1986. ML156.7.B77G3

Jazz Discographies Unlimited Presents Les Brown and his Band of Renown: A Discography. Whittier, CA: Jazz Discographies Unlimited, c1965. LCCN 82-229283. ML156.7.B77J4

Byrne, Bobby

  Garrod, Charles and Bill Korst. **Bobby Byrne and his Orchestra.** Zephyrhills, FL: Joyce Record Club Publication, 1992. LCCN 93-151539

Calloway, Cab

  Popa, Jay. **Cab Calloway and his Orchestra: 1925-1958.** rev. Zephyrhills, FL: Joyce Record Club Publication, 1987. LCCN 88-173127. ML156.7.C26P6

Carroll, Robert

  Evensmo, Jan. **The Tenor Saxophones of Henry Bridges, Robert Carroll, Herschal Evans, Johnny Russell: with a Critical Assessment of all their Known Records and Broadcasts.** Hosle, Norway: J. Evensmo, 1976. LCCN 82-210390. ML156.4.J3E93

Cash, Johnny

  Smith, John L. **The Johnny Cash Discography.** Westport, CT: Greenwood Press, 1985. LCCN 84-19799. ISBN 0-313-29167-5. ML156.7.C32S58

Cavallaro, Carmen

  Garrod, Charles. **Carmen Cavallaro and his Orchestra.** Zephyrhills, FL: Joyce Record Club, 1989. LCCN 90-164084. ML156.7.C34 G4

Chester, Bob

  Garrod, Charles. **Bob Chester and his Orchestra.** Rev. Zephyrhills, FL: Joyce Record Publication, 1987. LCCN 88-173122. ML156.7.C36G3

Christian, Charlie

  Evensmo, Jan. **The Guitars of Charlie Christian, Robert Normann, Oscar Aleman (in Europe).** Hosle, Norway: J. Evensmo, 1976 [?]. LCCN 84-211043. ML156.7.C4E9

Clapton, Eric

  Roberty, Marc. **Eric Clapton: The Complete Recording Sessions 1963-1992.** New York: St. Martin's Press, 1993. 192p.

ISBN 0-312-09798-0

Clark, Buddy

Garrod, Charles. **Buddy Clark**. Zephyrhills, FL: Joyce Record Club Publication, 1991. 44p. LCCN 92-195353. ML156.7.C47G3

Clinton, Larry

Garrod, Charles. **Larry Clinton and his Orchestra**. Rev. Zephyrhills, FL: Joyce Record Club Publications, 1990. LCCN 91-132198. ML156.7.C5G37

Cole, Nat "King"

Garrod, Charles. **Nat "King" Cole: His Voice and Piano**. Zephyrhills, FL: Joyce Record Club Publication, 1987. LCCN 87-402753. ML156.7.C57G37

Teubig, Klaus. **Straighten Up and Fly Right: A Chronology and Discography of Nat "King" Cole.** Westport, CT: Greenwood Press, 1994. ISBN 0-313-29251-5.

Coleman, Ornette

Wild, David Anthony and Michael Cuscuna. **Ornette Coleman, 1958-1979: a Discography.** Ann Arbor, MI: Wildmusic, 1980.

Coltrane, John

Fujioka, Yasuhiro, **John Coltrane: A Discography and Musical Biography**. Metuchen, NJ: Scarecrow Press, 1994.

Jepsen, Jorgen Grunnet. **A Discography of John Coltrane**. Copenhagen, NV: Karl Emil Knudsen, 1969. LCCN 73-452311. ML156.7.C58 J5

Wild, David Anthony. **The Recordings of John Coltrane: A Discography**. Ann Arbor, MI: Wildmusic, c1977. 72p. LCCN 78-305388. ML156.7.C58W5

Costello, Elvis

Parkyn, Geoff. **Elvis Costello: The Illustrated Disco/Biography**. London: Omnibus Press (distributed by New York: Cherry Lane Books), c1984. 80p. LCCN 86-228200. ML156.7.C62P3

Crosby, Bing

Morgereth, Timothy A. **Bing Crosby: A Discography, Radio Program List, and Filmography**. Jefferson, NC: McFarland, c1987. 554p. LCCN 85-43582. ML156.7.C7M67

Crosby, Bob

Garrod, Charles. **Bob Crosby and his Orchestra.** Zephyrhills, FL: Joyce Record Club, 1987. LCCN 88-167896. ML156.7.C75G3

Davis, Miles

Jepsen, Jorgen Grunnet. **A Discography of Miles Davis**. Copenhagen, NV: Karl Emil Knudsen, 1969. LCCN 72-452205. ML156.7.D4J4

Lohmann, Jan. **The Sound of Miles Davis, The Discography 1945-1991**. Copenhagen: JazzMedia, 1993. 396p. LCCN 93-169376. ISBN 8788043126

DeFranco, Buddy

Kuehn, John and Arne Astrup. **Buddy DeFranco: A Biographical Portrait and Discography.** Metuchen, NJ: Scarecrow Press; New Brunswick, NJ: Institute of Jazz Studies - Rutgers, 1993. 261p. LCCN 93-19962. ISBN 0-8108-2538-4

Diddly, Bo

White, George R. **The Complete Bo Diddly Sessions**. Bradford, England: G.R. White Publications, c1993. 92p. LCCN 93-154229. ISBN 0-9519888-0-8

Dolphy, Eric

Reichardt, Uwe. **Like a Human Voice: The Eric Dolphy Discography**. Schmitten, West Germany: N. Ruecker, 1986. LCCN 86-226462. ML156.7.D64R4

Donahue, Al

Garrod, Charles. **Al Donahue and his Orchestra. Van Alexander and his Orchestra**. Zephyrhills, FL: Joyce Record Club Publication, 1991. LCCN 93-167129

Donahue, Sam

> Garrod, Charles. **Sam Donahue and his Orchestra**.
> Zephyrhills, FL: Joyce Record Club Publication, 1992. 21p.
> LCCN 92-195313. ML156.7.D65G3

The Dorsey Brothers

> Garrod, Charles. **The Dorsey Brothers and their Orchestra**.
> Zephyrhills, FL: Joyce Record Club Publication, 1992. LCCN 93-
> 151553

Dorsey, Jimmy

> Garrod, Charles. **Jimmy Dorsey and his Orchestra.** Rev.
> Zephyrhills, FL: Joyce Record Club Publication, 1988. LCCN 88-
> 178236. ML156.7.D66G3

> **Jazz Discographies Unlimited Presents Jimmy Dorsey and
> his Orchestra: A Complete Discography Covering the
> Years 1935 to 1957, Listing all Commercial Recordings,
> Transcriptions, Airchecks, Unissued Titles, and all Band
> Personnel, Recording and Non-recording**. Whittier, CA:
> ErnGeoBil Publications, 1966. LCCN 82-222280. ML156.7.D66J4

Dorsey, Tommy

> Garrod, Charles. **Tommy Dorsey and his Orchestra**. Rev.
> Zephyrhills, FL: Joyce Record Club, 1988. LCCN 88-169725.
> ML156.7.D67G3

The Drifters

> Allan, Tony and Faye Treadwell. **Save the Last Dance for Me:
> The Musical Legacy of the Drifters, 1953-1993**. 220p. Ann
> Arbor, MI: Popular Culture, Ink, 1993. LCCN 92-81113. ISBN 1-
> 56075-028-6

Duchin, Eddy

> Garrod, Charles. **Eddy Duchin and his Orchestra.**
> Zephyrhills, FL: Joyce Record Club Publication, 1989. LCCN 90-
> 164556. ML156.7.D8G4

Dunham, Sonny

> Garrod, Charles. **Sonny Dunhan and his Orchestra. Ziggy
> Elman and his Orchestra**. Zephyrhills, FL: Joyce Record Club

Publication, 1990. LCCN 93-169830

Dylan, Bob

Cable, Paul. **Bob Dylan: His Unreleased Recordings**. 1st American ed. New York: Schirmer Books, 1980. 197p. LCCN 79-57285. ML156.7.D97C3

Dorman, James E. **Recorded Dylan: A Critical Review and Discography**. 1st ed. Pinedale, CA: Soma Press of California, c1982. 123p. LCCN 82-60706. ML156.7.D97D7

Hoggard, Stuart. **Bob Dylan: An Illustrated Discography**. Oxford: Transmedia Express, 1978. LCCN 78-321075. ML156.7.D97 H6

Krogsgaard, Michael. **Positively Bob Dylan: A Thirty-Year Discography, Concert & Recording Session Guide, 1960-1991**. Ann Arbor, MI: Popular Culture, Ink, 1991.

Eddy, Nelson

Kiner, Larry F. **Nelson Eddy: A Bio-Discography**. Metuchen, NJ: Scarecrow Press, 1992. 683p. LCCN 92-1232. ML156.7.E2K5

Edwards, Cliff

Kiner, Larry F. **The Cliff Edwards Discography**. Westport, CT: Greenwood Press, 1987. 260p. LCCN 86-31798. ML156.7.E3K5

Elgart, Les and Larry Elgart

Garrod, Charles. **Les and Larry Elgart and their Orchestra**. Rev. Zephyrhills, FL: Joyce Record Club Publication, 1992. LCCN 93-151535.

Ellington, Duke

Moule, Francois-Xavier. **The Duke Ellington Recorded Legacy on LPs and CDs, Volume I**. Le Mans, France: Madley Productions, 1993. 684p.

Timner, W. E. **Ellingtonia: The Recorded Music of Duke Ellington and his Sidemen**. 3rd ed. Metuchen, NJ: Institute of Jazz Studies/Scarecrow Press, 1988. 534p. LCCN 86-21967. ML156.5.E45T5

Valburn, Jerry. **Duke Ellington on Compact Disc**. Hicksville, NY: Marlor Productions (P.O. Box 156, Hicksville, NY 11803), 1993. 258p.

Elman, Ziggy

Garrod, Charles. **Sonny Dunhan and his Orchestra**. Ziggy Elman and his Orchestra. Zephyrhills, FL: Joyce Record Club Publication, 1990. LCCN 93-169830

Evans, Gil

Tajiri, Tetsuya. **Gil Evans Discography, 1941-1982**. Tokyo: T. Tajiri, 1983.

Evans, Herschal

Evensmo, Jan. **The Tenor Saxophones of Henry Bridges, Robert Carroll, Herschal Evans, Johnny Russell: With a Critical Assessment of all their Known Records and Broadcasts**. Hosle, Norway: J. Evensmo, 1976. LCCN 82-210390. ML156.4.J3E93

Everly Brothers

Hosum, John. **Living Legends: The Everly Brothers: The history of the Everly Brothers on Record: An Illustrated Discography**. Seattle, WA: Foreverly Music, c1985. 64p. LCCN 84-90525. ML156.7.E9H7

Fields, Shep

Garrod, Charles. **Shep Fields and his Orchestra**. Zephyrhills, FL: Joyce Record Club Publication, 1987. ML156.7.F53G4

Fio Rito, Ted

Garrod, Charles. **Ted Fio Rito and his Orchestra; Plus, Ina Ray Hutton and her Orchestra**. Zephyrhills, FL: Joyce Record Club, 1988. LCCN 90-166252. ML156.7.F56G3

Flanagan, Ralph

Garrod, Charles. **Ralph Flanagan and his Orchestra**. Rev. Zephyrhills, FL: Joyce Record Club Publication, 1990. LCCN 91-132189. ML156.7.F62G3

Florence, Bob

Wolfer, Jurgen. **Si Zentner and his Orchestra, also includ-
ing Bob Florence and his Orchestra: A Discography**.
Zephyrhills, FL: Joyce Music Publication, [?]. LCCN 87-119995.
ML156.4.B5W6

Forrest, Helen

Garrod, Charles. **Helen Forest**. Zephyrhills, FL: Joyce Record
Club Publication, 1993. LCCN 93-151570

Foster, Chuck

Garrod, Charles. **Chuck Foster and his Orchestra**.
Zephyrhills, FL: Joyce Record Club Publication, 1992. 31p.
LCCN 92-195259. ML156.7.F7G3

Garber, Lan

Garrod, Charles. **Jan Garber and his Orchestra**.
Zephyrhills, FL: Joyce Record Club Publication, 1992. LCCN 93-
151555

Getz, Stan

Astrup, Arne. **The Revised Stan Getz Discography**. 3d ed.
Karlslunde, Denmark: Per Meistrup Productions Co., 1991.

Gillespie, Dizzy

Jepsen, Jorgen Grunnet. **A Discography of Dizzy Gillespie**.
Copenhagen: Karl Emil Knudsen, 1969. 2v. LCCN 73-576411.
ML156.7.G54J5

Koster, Piet and Chris Sellers. **Dizzy Gillespie**. Amsterdam:
Micrography, 1985-1988.

Goodman, Benny

Connor, D. Russell. **Benny Goodman: Listen to his Legacy**.
Metuchen, NJ: Scarecrow Press and the Institute of Jazz Studies,
1988. 357p. LCCN 87-32069. ML156.7.G66C57

Gordon, Dexter

Sjogren, Thorbjorn. **Long Tall Dexter: The Discography of**

Dexter Gordon. Copenhagen: T. Sjogren, 1986.

Gray, Glen

　　Garrod, Charles and Bill Korst. **Glen Gray and the Casa Loma Orchestra**. Zephyrhills, FL: Joyce Record Club Publication, 1993. LCCN 93-140692

Gray, Jerry

　　Popa, Chris. **Jerry Gray and his Orchestra**. Zephyrhills, FL: Joyce Music, 1984. LCCN 87-121612. ML156.7.G72P6

Handy, George

　　Garrod, Charles. **Boyd Raeburn and his Orchestra, Plus Johnny Bothwell and George Handy**. Zephyrhills, FL: Joyce Music, 1985. LCCN 87-121644. ML156.7.R33G3

Hawkins, Coleman

　　Chilton, John. **The Song of the Hawk: The Life and Recordings of Coleman Hawkins.** Ann Arbor: University of Michigan Press, 1993.

　　Evensmo, Jan. **The Tenor Saxophone of Coleman Hawkins, 1929-1942: with a Critical Assessment of all his Known Records and Broadcasts.** Rev. ed. Hosle, Norway: the Author, 1975[?] 33 p. LCCN 76-374187. ML156.7.H35E9

Hawkins, Erskine

　　Garrod, Charles. **Erskine Hawkins and his Orchestra.** Zephyrhills, FL: Joyce Record Club Publication, 1992. 17p. LCCN 92-195267. ML156.7.H36G3

Haymes, Dick

　　Garrod, Charles. **Dick Haymes**. Zephyrhills, FL: Joyce Record Club, 1990. LCCN 91-131699. ML156.7.H37G4

Heidt, Horace

　　Garrod, Charles. **Horace Heidt and his Orchestra**. Zephyrhills, FL: Joyce Record Club Publication, 1993. LCCN 93-203995.

Henderson, Fletcher

> Allen, Walter C. **Hendersonia: The Music of Fletcher Henderson and his Musicians**. Highland Park, NJ: 1973. 651p. LCCN 72-85818. ML156.7.H45A4

Hendrix, Jimi

> Matesich, Ken. **Jimi Hendrix: A Discography**. 1st ed., rev. Tucson, AZ: Purple Haze Archives (P.O. Box 41133, Tucson 85717), 1982. 53p. LCCN 84163260. ML156.7.H47M4

Herman, Woody

> Garrod, Charles. **Woody Herman and his Orchestra**. Zephyrhills, FL: Joyce Record Club Publication, 1985-1988. 3 v. LCCN 87-124083. ML156.7.H49G4

> Morrill, Dexter. **Woody Herman: A Guide to the Big Band Recordings, 1936-1987**. Westport, CT: Greenwood Press, 1990. 129 p. LCCN 90-13989. ML156.7.H49M7

> Treichel, James A. **Keeper of the Flame: Woody Herman and the Second Herd, 1947-1949**. Zephyrhillis, FL: Joyce Music Publication, 1978. LCCN 87-119984. ML156.7.H49T7

Hill, Tiny

> Garrod, Charles. **Tiny Hill and his Orchestra**. Zephyrhills, FL: Joyce Record Club Publication, 1992. LCCN 93-151547

Hines, Earl

> Moxhet, Lionel. **A Discography of Earl Hines, 1923-1977: Records, Festivals and Concerts**. Sannois, France: L. Moxhet, 1982.

Holiday, Billie

> Jepsen, Jorgen Grunnet. **A Discography of Billie Holiday**. Copenhagen: K.E. Knudsen, [?].

> Millar, Jack. **Born to Sing: A Discography of Billie Holiday**. Copenhagen: Jazzmedia, 1979.

Holly, Buddy

> Griggs, Bill. **Buddy Holly: A Collectors Guide**. Sheboygan,

WI (P.O. Box 596, Sheboygan 53081): Red Wax Pub. Co., c1983. 92p. LCCN 84-170068. ML156.7.H63G7

Howard, Eddy

Garrod, Charles. **Eddy Howard and his Orchestra.** Zephyrhills, FL: Joyce Record Club Publication, 1991. 41p. LCCN 93-169799

Hutton, Ina Ray

Garrod, Charles. **Ted Fio Rito and his Orchestra; plus, Ina Ray Hutton and her Orchestra.** Zephyrhills, FL: Joyce Record Club, 1988. LCCN 90-166252. ML156.7.F56G3

Jackson, Michael

Terry, Carol D. **Sequins and Shades: The Michael Jackson Reference Guide.** Ann Arbor, MI: Pierian Press, 1987.

James, Harry

Garrod, Charles. **Harry James and his Orchestra.** Zephyrhills, FL: Joyce Music Publications, 1985. 3 v. LCCN 87-124051. ML156.7.J34G4

Jazz Discographies Unlimited Presents Harry James and his Orchestra. Whittier, CA: Jazz Discographies Unlimited, 1971. LCCN 82-226843. ML156.7.J34J4

John, Elton

Distefano, John. **The Complete Elton John Discography.** New Baltimore, MI (Box 760, New Baltimore 48047): East End Lights, c1993. 66p. LCCN 93-173684

Jolson, Al

Kiner, Larry F. **Al Jolson: A Bio-Discography.** Metuchen, NJ: Scarecrow Press, 1992. 808p. LCCN 92-40029. ISBN 0-8108-2633-X. ML156.7.J64K4

Kiner, Larry F. **The Al Jolson Discography.** Westport, CT: Greenwood Press, 1983. 194p. LCCN 83-12813. ML156.7.J64K5

Jones, Isham

Garrod, Charles. **Isham Jones and his Orchestra.**

Zephyrhills, FL: Joyce Record Club Publication, 1992. LCCN 93-204032

Jones, Spike

Mirtle, Jack. **Thank You Music Lovers: A Bio-Discography of Spike Jones and his City Slickers, 1941 to 1965**. Westport, CT: Greenwood Press, 1986. 426p. LCCN 85-27128. ML156.7.J66M6

Jordan, Duke

Sjogren, Thorbjorn. **The Discography of Duke Jordan**. Copenhagen: Thorbjorn Sjogren, 1982. 52p. LCCN 82-502697. ML156.7.J67S6

Kaye, Sammy

Sammy Kaye and his Orchestra. Zephyrhills, FL: Joyce Record   Club   Publication,   1988.   LCCN   88-171059. ML156.7.K38G4

Kemp, Hal

Garrod, Charles. **Hal Kemp and his Orchestra**. Zephyrhills, FL: Joyce Record Club Publication, 1990. LCCN 91-101801. ML156.7.K43G4

Kenton, Stan

Garrod, Charles.   **Stan Kenton and his Orchestra**. Zephyrhills, FL: Joyce Music Publications, 1984-1991. 3 v. LCCN 87-117524. ML156.7.K45G3

Jazz Discographies Unlimited Presents the Great Kenton Arrangers: Bill Holman, Gene Roland ... et al. Whittier, CA: ErnGeoBil Publications, 1968. LCCN 82-229293. ML156.7.H64 J4

Sparke, Michael, Pete Venudor and Jack Hartley. **Kenton on Capitol: a Discography.** Hounslow Middlesex, Eng.: Michael Sparke, [1967]

The King Sisters

Garrod, Charles. **Alvino Rey and his Orchestra, Plus the King Sisters, 1939-1958**. Zephyrhills, FL: Joyce Music Studio, 1986. LCCN 87-119936. ML156.7.R49G4

Kirby, John

   Garrod, Charles. **John Kirby and his Orchestra; Andy Kirk
   and his orchestra**.   Zephyrhills, FL: Joyce Record Club
   Publication, 1991. LCCN 92-195273. ML156.7.K52G3

Kirk, Andy

   Garrod, Charles. **John Kirby and his Orchestra; Andy Kirk
   and his Orchestra**.   Zephyrhills, FL: Joyce Record Club
   Publication, 1991. LCCN 92-195273. ML156.7.K52G3

Krupa, Gene

   Garrod,   Charles.   **Gene   Krupa   and   his   Orchestra**.
   Zephyrhills, FL: Joyce Music Publications, 1984. 2 v. LCCN 87-
   117449. ML156.7.K78G4

   Hall, George I. **Gene Krupa and his Orchestra**. Laurel, MD:
   Jazz Discographies Unlimited, 1975. 90p.   LCCN 75-19346.
   ML156.7.K78 H3

Kyser, Kay

   Garrod, Charles and Bill Korst. **Kay Kyser and his Orchestra**.
   Zephyrhills, FL: Joyce Record Club Publication, 1992.   rev.
   LCCN 93-151558

Lawrence, Elliot

   Garrod, Charles. **Elliot Lawrence and his Orchestra**. rev.
   Zephyrhills, FL: Joyce Record Club Publication, 1986.
   ML156.7.L38G4

Lee, Peggy

   Towe,   Ronald.   **Here's To You: The Complete Bio-
   Discography of Miss Peggy Lee**. San Francisco, CA: R. Towe
   Music, c1986. 542p. LCCN 87-107262. ML156.7.L43T7

Little Richard

   Garodkin, John. **Little Richard, King of Rock 'n' Roll**.
   Copenhagen: C. P. Wulff, 1975.   71 p.   LCCN 76-374186.
   ML156.7.L57G4

Long, Johnny

> Garrod, Charles. **Johnny Long and his Orchestra**. rev. Zephyrhills, FL: Joyce Record Club Publications, 1989. LCCN 90-167463. ML156.7.L66 4

Lunceford, Jimmie

> Garrod, Charles. **Jimmie Lunceford and his Orchestra.** Zephyrhills, FL: Joyce Record Club Publication, 1990. 27p. LCCN 93-169813

Marterie, Ralph

> Brethour, Ross. **Ralph Materie and his Orchestra**. Zephyrhills, FL: Joyce Record Club Publication, 1992. LCCN 92-195298. ML156.7.M27B7

Martin, Freddy

> Garrod, Charles. **Freddy Martin and his Orchestra**. Zephyrhills, FL: Joyce Record Club Publication, 1987. LCCN 88-173138. ML156.7.M3G3

Masters, Frankie

> Garrod, Charles. **Frankie Masters and his Orchestra**. Zephyrhills, FL: Joyce Record Club, 1989. LCCN 90-166266. ML156.7.M33G37

May, Billy

> Garrod, Charles. **Billy May and his Orchestra**. Zephyrhills, FL: Joyce Record Club Publication, 1991. 39p. LCCN 93-167208

McKinley, Ray

> **Ray McKinley and his Orchestra.** Zephyrhills, FL: Joyce Music Publications, 1979. LCCN 87-123045. ML156.7.M36P6

McKinney's Cotton Pickers

> Chilton, John. **McKinney's Music: A Bio-Discography of McKinney's Cotton Pickers**. London: Bloomsbury Book Shop, 1978.

Miller, Glenn

Flower, John. **Moonlight Serenade: A Bio-Discography of the Glenn Miller Civilian Band.** New Rochelle, NY: Arlington House 1972. 554 p. LCCN 74-179717. ML156.7.M5F6

Garrod, Celeste D. and Charles Garrod. **The Ajazz Glenn Miller Lives Series Companion.** Zephyrhills, FL: Zephyr Music Corp, 1992. LCCN 93-143298

Millinder, Lucky

Discography of Lucky Millinder. Basel (Postfach 736, Basel1): Jazz-Publications, 1962. 26p. LCCN 81-467673. ML156.7.M53D6

Mingus, Charles

Ruppli, Michel. **Charles Mingus Discography**. Frankfurt: N. Ruecker, 1981, c1982. 47p. LCCN 83-137676. ML156.7.M56R86

Monk, Thelonious

Jepsen, Jorgen Grunnet. **A Discography of Thelonious Monk and Bud Powell.** Copenhagen: Karl Emil Knudsen 1969 LCCN 75-452045. ML156.7.M65J5

Monroe, Bill

Rosenberg, Neil V. **Bill Monroe and his Blue Grass Boys**. Nashville: Country Music Foundation Press, c1974. 122p. LCCN 77-350343. ML156.7.M66R7

Monroe, Vaughn

Garrod, Charles. **Vaughn Monroe and his Orchestra**. Zephyrhills, FL: Joyce Record Club Publication, 1986. LCCN 88-173133. ML156.7.M663G4

Morgan, Russ

Garrod, Charles. **Russ Morgan and his Orchestra**. Zephyrhills, FL: Joyce Record Club Publication, 1993. LCCN 93-204628.

Morton, Jelly Roll

Hill, Michael. **Jelly Roll Morton: A Microgroove**

Appendix A: Individual Discographies

Discography and Musical Analysis. Salisbury East, Australia: Salisbury College of Advanced Education, 1977.

Mulligan, Gerry

Astrup, Arnie. **The Gerry Mulligan Discography**. Denmark: Bidstrup Discographical Publishing, [?]. 106p.

Nelson, Ozzie

Garrod, Charles. **Ozzie Nelson and his Orchestra**. Zephyrhills, FL: Joyce Record Club Publication, 1991. 18p. LCCN 92-195293. ML156.7.N44G3

Nelson, Willie

Bartlett, Colleen. **Willie Nelson: Official Discography**. Dorset, VT (P.O. Box 158, Dorset 05251): C. Bartlett, c1990. LCCN 91-108150. ML156.7.N47B3

Noble, Ray

Garrod, Charles. **Ray Noble and His Orchestra**. Zephyrhills, FL: Joyce Record Club Publication, 1991. 66p. LCCN 92-195307. ML156.7.N62G3

O'Day, Anita

Wolfer, Jurgen. **Anita O'Day: An Exploratory Discography.** Zephyrhills, FL: Joyce Record Club Publication, 1990. LCCN 90-175426. ML156.7.O32W6

Oliver, Sy

Garrod, Charles. **Sy Oliver and his Orchestra**. Zephyrhills, FL: Joyce Record Club Publication, 1993. LCCN 93-204631

Osbourne, Will

Garrod, Charles. **Will Osborne and his Orchestra**. Zephyrhills, FL: Joyce Record Club Publication, 1991. 22p. LCCN 92-195319. ML156.7.O82G3

Parker, Charlie

Bregman, Robert, Leonard Bukowski and Norman Saks. **The**

Charlie Parker Discography. Redwood, NY: Cadence Jazz Books, c1993.

Jepsen, Jorgen Grunnet. **A Discography of Charlie Parker**. Copenhagen NV: Karl Emil Knudsen, 1968. LCCN 71-452517. ML156.7.P35 J4

Koch, Lawrence O. **Yardbird Suite: A Compendium of the Music and Life of Charlie Parker**. Bowling Green, OH: Bowling Green State University Popular Press, c1988. 336p. LCCN 88-73435. ML156.7.P35K6

Koster, Piet and Dick M. Bakker. **Charlie Parker**. Alphen aan den Rijn, Holland: Micrography, 1974-1976.

Pastor, Tony

Garrod, Charles. **Tony Pastor and his Orchestra**. Zephyrhills, FL: Joyce Music Studio Publication, 1986. ML156.7.P363G3

Pepper, Art

Edwards, Ernest. **Art Pepper: A Complete Discography**. Whittier, CA: Jazz Discographies Unlimited, 1965.

Pettiford, Oscar

Gazdar, Coover. **First Bass: The Oscar Pettiford Discography.** Rydal, FL: David Goldenberg (840 Winter Road), 1992. 110p.

Powell, Bud

Jepsen, Jorgen Grunnet. **A Discography of Thelonious Monk and Bud Powell.** Copenhagen: Karl Emil Knudsen, 1969 LCCN 75-452045. ML156.7.M65J5

Powell, Teddy

Garrod, Charles. **Teddy Powell and his Orchestra**. rev. Zephyrhills, FL: Joyce Record Club Publication, 1990. LCCN 90-172853. ML156.7.P65G4

Presley, Elvis

Aros, Andrew A. **Elvis, his Films & Recordings**. Diamond Bar, CA: Applause Publications, c1980. 64p. LCCN 79-55876. ML156.7.P7A8

Banney, Howard F. **Return to Sender: The First Complete Discography of Elvis, Tribute & Novelty Records, 1956-1986**. Ann Arbor, MI: Pierian Press, 1987. 318p. LCCN 87-61977. ML156.4.P6B35

Barry, Ron. **The Elvis Presley American Discography**. Phillipsburg, NJ: Spectator Service, Maxigraphics, 1976.

Cotten, Lee. **Jailhouse Rock: The Bootleg Records of Elvis Presley, 1970-1983**. Ann Arbor, MI: Pierian Press, 1983. 367p. LCCN 83-61755. ML156.7.P7C67

Jorgensen, Ernst. **Reconsider Baby: The Definitive Elvis Sessionography, 1954-1977.** 1986 repr. ed. with additions. Ann Arbor, MI: Pierian Press, 1986. 308p. LCCN 86-61746. ML156.7.P7J7

Sauers, Wendy. **Elvis Presley, a Complete Reference: Biography, Chronology, Concerts List, Filmography, Discography, Vital Documents, Bibliography, Index.** Jefferson, NC: McFarland, 1984.

Townson, John. **Elvis-UK: The Ultimate Guide to Elvis Presley's British Record Releases, 1956-1985.** Poole, England: Blandford Press (distributed by New York: Sterling), 1987. 565p. LCCN 86-166518. ML156.7.P7T68

Tunzi, Joseph A. **Elvis Sessions: The Recorded Music of Elvis Aron Presley, 1953-1977**. Chicago: Jat Productions. c1993. 347p. LCCN 93-91504. ISBN 0-9620083-5-4

Umphred, Neal. **Elvis: A Touch of Gold, the American Record Collector's Price Guide to Elvis Presley Records & Memorabilia.** 1st ed. Saugus, CA (Box 130, Saugus 91350): White Dragon Press, 1990. 326p. LCCN 89-51912. ML156.7.P7U4

Umphred, Neal. **Elvis Presley.** Phoenix, AZ: O'Sullivan Woodside (Distributed by Caroline House), c1985. 173p. LCCN 85-21729. ML156.7.P7U46

Whisler, John A. **Elvis Presley, Reference Guide and Discography**. Metuchen, NJ: Scarecrow Press, 1981.

Prima, Louis

Garrod, Charles. **Louis Prima and his Orchestra.** Zephyrhills, FL: Joyce Record Club Publication, 1991. 31p. LCCN 93-167226

Raeburn, Boyd

> Garrod, Charles. **Boyd Raeburn and his Orchestra, plus Johnny Bothwell and George Handy.** Zephyrhills, FL: Joyce Music, 1985. LCCN 87-121644. ML156.7.R33G3

Rey, Alvino

> Garrod, Charles. **Alvino Rey and his Orchestra, plus the King Sisters, 1939-1958**. Zephyrhills, FL: Joyce Music Studio, 1986. LCCN 87-119936. ML156.7.R49G4

Rich, Buddy

> Meriwether, Doug. **We Don't Play Requests: A Musical Biography/Discography of Buddy Rich**. Chicago, IL: Distributed by KAR Publications, c1984. 234p. LCCN 83-90193. ML156.7.R5M5

Richard, Cliff

> Lewry, Peter. **Cliff Richard: The Complete Recording Sessions, 1958-1990**. London: Blandford (Distributed by New York: Sterling Pub. Co.), 1991. 191p. LCCN 92-131562. ML156.7.R54L5

Rodgers, Jimmie

> Bond, Johnny. **The Recordings of Jimmie Rodgers: An Annotated Discography**. Los Angeles: John Edwards Memorial Foundation, c1978. 76p. LCCN 79-124607. ML156.7.R62B6

The Rolling Stones

> Aeppli, Felix. **Heart of Stone: The Definitive Rolling Stones Discography, 1962-1983**. Ann Arbor, MI: Pierian Press, 1985. 535p. LC 85-60592. ML156.7.R66 A35

> Elliott, Martin. **The Rolling Stones: Complete Recording Sessions, 1963-1989: A Sessionography, Discography, and History of Recordings from the Famous Chart-Toppers to the Infamous Rarities, January 1963-November 1989**. London: Blandford (distributed by New York: Sterling Pub. Co.), 1990. 223 p. LCCN 90-197644. ML156.7.R66E4

> Miles, Barry. **The Rolling Stones: An Illustrated Discography**. London: Omnibus Press, 1980.

Rollins, Sonny

> Sjogren, Thorbjorn. **The Sonny Rollins Discography.**
> Copenhagen: T. Sjogren, 1983.

Russell, Johnny

> Evensmo, Jan. **The Tenor Saxophones of Henry Bridges,
> Robert Carroll, Herschal Evans, Johnny Russell: With a
> Critical Assessment of all their Known Records and
> Broadcasts**. Hosle, Norway: J. Evensmo, 1976. LCCN 82-
> 210390. ML156.4.J3E93

Russell, Pee Wee

> Hilbert, Robert. **Pee Wee Speaks: A Discography of Pee Wee
> Russell**. Metuchen, NJ: Scarecrow Press, 1992. 377 p. LCCN
> 92-37522. ML156.7.R88H5

Savitt, Jan

> Hall, George I. **Jan Savitt and his Orchestra**. rev. by Charles
> Garrod. Zephyrhills, FL: Joyce Music Studio, 1985. LCCN 87-
> 121604. ML156.7.S28 H3

> **Jazz Discographies Unlimited Presents Jan Savitt and his
> Top Hatters: A Complete Discography Covering the Entire
> Recording History of this Fine Orchestra**. Whittier, CA:
> ErnGeoBil Publications, 1966. LCCN 82-229266.
> ML156.7.S28J4

Scott, Raymond

> Garrod, Charles. **Raymond Scott and his Orchestra**.
> Zephyrhills, FL: Joyce Record Club Publication, 1988. LCCN 89-
> 101519. ML156.7.S38G47

Shaw, Artie

> Korst, William. **Artie Shaw and his Orchestra**. Zephyrhills,
> FL: Joyce Music Publication, 1986. ML156.7.S47K7

Sherwood, Bobby

> Garrod, Charles. **Bobby Sherwood and his Orchestra;
> Randy Brooks and his Orchestra**. Zephyrhills, FL: Joyce
> Record Club Publication, 1987. LCCN 88-173112.
> ML156.7.S5G4

Sims, Zoot

Astrup, Arne. **The John Haley Sims (Zoot Sims) Disco-graphy**. Lyngby Denmark: Dansk Historisk Handbogsforlag, c1980.

Sinatra, Frank

Ackelson, Richard W. **Frank Sinatra: A Complete Recording History of Techniques, Songs, Composers, Lyricists, Arrangers, Sessions, and First-Issue Albums, 1939-1984**. Jefferson, NC: McFarland, c1992.   466p.   LCCN 91-52629. ML156.7.S56A25

Garrod, Charles. **Frank Sinatra.**   Zephyrhills, FL: Joyce Record Club Publication, 1989-1990.   LCCN 90-174351. ML156.7.S56G4

Lonstein, Albert I. and Vito Marino. **The Revised Complete Sinatra: Discography,   Filmography,   Television Appearances,   Motion   Picture   Appearances,   Radio Appearances, Concert Appearances, Stage Appearances**. Ellenville, NY: S.M. Lonstein, 1979.

Sayers, Scott P. and Ed O'Brien. **Sinatra: The Man and his Music, the Recording Artistry of Francis Albert Sinatra, 1939-1992.** Austin, TX: TSD Press, c1992. 303p. LCCN 93-176766. ISBN 0-934367-24-8

Slack, Freddie

Garrod, Charles. **Will Bradley and his Orchestra; plus, Freddie Slack and his Orchestra.** Zephyrhills, FL: Joyce Music Publication, 1986. LCCN 87-119948. ML156.7.B72G4

Sparks, Larry

Petersen, Henning. **Larry Sparks and the Lonesome Ramblers: A Discography with Songs & Notes on Guitarstyle [sic]**. Harlev, Denmark : H. Petersen, 1988. 32 p. LCCN 92-788983. ML156.4.C7P48

Spivak, Charlie

Garrod, Charles. **Charlie Spivak and his Orchestra.** Zephyrhills, FL: Joyce Music Publication, 1986.   LCCN 87-

119932. ML156.7.S7G3

Jazz Discographies Unlimited Presents Charlie Spivak and his Orchestra. Whittier, CA: JDU, 1972. LCCN 82-226990. ML156.7.S7J4

Stanley, Ralph

Wright, John. **Ralph Stanley & the Clinch Mountain Boys: A Discography.** Evanston, IL (1137 Noyes St., Evanston 60201): J. Wright, 1983[?]. LCCN 84-227794. ML156.7.S78W7

Tatum, Art

Laubich, Arnold. **Art Tatum: A Guide to his Recorded Music.** Newark, NJ: Institute of Jazz Studies, Rutgers University; Metuchen, NJ: Scarecrow Press, 1982. 330p. LCCN 82-10752. ML156.7.T37L4

Thornhill, Claude

Garrod, Charles. **Claude Thornhill and his Orchestra.** Zephyrhills, FL: Joyce Music Publication, 1985. LCCN 87-119990. ML156.7.T5G4

Tristano, Lenny

Susat, Jurgen W. **Discography of the "Uncompromising Lennie Tristano."** Menden: Der Jazzfreund, c1986. LCCN 90-111897. ML156.7.T74S9

Trumbauer, Frank

Evans, Philip R. and Larry F. Kiner. **Tram: The Frank Trumbauer Story, a Bio-Discography.** Metuchen, NJ: Scarecrow Press, 1994.

Tucker, Orrin

Garrod, Charles. **Orrin Tucker and his Orchestra.** Zephyrhills, FL: Joyce Record Club Publication, 1992. 18p. LCCN 92-195277. ML156.7.T826G3

Tucker, Tommy

Garrod, Charles. **Tommy Tucker and his Orchestra.** Zephyrhills, FL: Joyce Record Club, 1990. LCCN 91-103308.

ML156.7.T83G3

Vallee, Rudy

Kiner, Larry F. **The Rudy Vallee Discography.** Westport, CT: Greenwood Press, 1985. 190p. LCCN 84-22491. ML156.7.V34K5

Vaughan, Sarah

Brown, Denis. **Sarah Vaughan: A Discography**. New York: Greenwood Press, 1991. 166p. LCCN 91-27632. ML156.7.V4B7

Waters, Muddy

Wight, Phil and Fred Rothwell. **The Complete Muddy Waters Discography.** Cheadle, Cheshire: Blues & Rhythm, 1991. 70p. LCCN 92-217639

Webster, Ben

Evensmo, Jan. **The Tenor Saxophone of Ben Webster, 1931-1943.** Hosle, Norway: J. Evensmo, 1978. 50p. LCCN 83-219100. ML156.7.W4E9

Weems, Ted

Garrod, Charles. **Ted Weems and His Orchestra.** Zephyrhills, FL: Joyce Record Club, 1990.   25 p.   LCCN 90-190057. ML156.4.P6G38

Young, Lester

Buchmann-Moller, Frank. **You Got to Be Original, Man: The Music of Lester Young.** New York: Greenwood Press, c1990. 52 p. LCCN 89-11986. ISBN 0-313-26514-3. ML156.7.Y7B8

Evensmo, Jan. **The Tenor Saxophone and Clarinet of Lester Young, 1936-1942: With a Critical Assessment of all his Known Records and Broadcasts**.   Hosle, Norway: Evensmo, 1977[?] 35p. LCCN 78-304246. ML156.7.Y7E9

Jepsen, Jorgen Grunnet. **A Discography of Lester Young.** Copenhagen: Karl Emil Knudsen, Dortheavej 39, 1968. LCCN 78-452516. ML156.7.Y7J4

Zentner, Si

Wolfer, Jurgen. **Si Zentner and his Orchestra, also including Bob Florence and his Orchestra: A Discography.** Zephyrhills, FL: Joyce Music Publication, [?]. LCCN 87-119995. ML156.4.B5W6

Appendix B: Individual Bibliographies

Baez, Joan

> Swanekamp, Joan. **Diamonds and Rust: A Bibliography and Discography on Joan Baez.** Ann Arbor, MI: Pieran Press, 1980.

The Beatles

> McKeen, William. **The Beatles: A Bio-Bibliography**. New York: Greenwood Press, 1989. 181p. LCCN 89-2219. ML421.B4 M3 1989

Braxton, Anthony

> Wachtmeister, Hans. **A Discography & Bibliography of Anthony Braxton**. Stocksund, Sweden: Blue Anchor, c1982. LC 86-228200. ML156.7.B738 W2 1982

Dylan, Bob

> McKeen, William. **Bob Dylan: A Bio-Bibliography**. Westport, CT: Greenwood Press, 1993. 307p. LCCN 92-32212. ML420.D98 M25 1993

Jackson, Michael

> Terry, Carol D. **Sequins and Shades: The Michael Jackson Reference Guide**. Ann Arbor, MI: Pierian Press, 1987. 507p..

Jolson, Al

> Fisher, James. **Al Jolson: A Bio-Bibliography**. Westport, CT: Greenwood Press, 1994. 321p..

Merman, Ethel

> Bryan, George B.   **Ethel Merman: A Bio-Bibliography**.
> Westport, CT: Greenwood Press, 1992. 298p..

Presley, Elvis

> Hammontree, Patsy Guy. **Elvis Presley: A Bio-Bibliography**.
> Westport, CT: Greenwood Press, 1985. 301p. LCCN 84-12773.
> ML420.P96H35

> Sauers, Wendy.   **Elvis Presley, a Complete Reference:
> Biography, Chronology, Concerts List, Filmography,
> Discography, Vital Documents, Bibliography, Index**.
> Jefferson, NC: McFarland, 1984.   194p.   LCCN 84-789.
> ML420.P96S28

The Who

> Wolter, Stephen.   **The Who in Print: An Annotated
> Bibliography, 1965 through 1990**.   Jefferson, NC:
> McFarland,1992. 154p. LCCN 92-50325. ISBN 0-89950-689-5.
> ML134.5.W5W64

Wilder, Alec

> Demsey, David and Ronald Prather.   **Alec Wilder: A Bio-
> Bibliography.** Westport, CT: Greenwood Press, 1993. 274p..

Williams, Hank

> Koon, George William. **Hank Williams: A Bio-Bibliography.**
> Westport, CT: Greenwood Press, 1983. 180p. LCCN 82-24162.
> ML420.W55K7

Appendix C: Electronic Resources

Indexes to Periodicals

Billboard Online.   New York: Billboard Electronic Publishing.
DOS/Win/Mac.

An online information service, available by subscription through
dial-in access (by modem).   It offers indexing and full text articles
from Billboard magazine from 1991 to the current issue.   It also
includes an archive of Billboard chart information, RIAA gold/-
platinum certification information, and a database of production
credits for music videos.

Indexes to Printed and Recorded Music

**The Grammys: 35 Years of the Best Performances on CD-
ROM**. New York: Mindscape. Mac.

A multimedia tour of the Grammy Awards. Searchable by
nominees and winners.   It includes biographies, photos, interviews, and 40 Quick-time movies.

Directories

Sourcebase: The Electronic Sourcebook.   Annual.   Los
Angeles, CA: Ascona Communications,. DOS/Mac.

An electronic version of the Recording Industry Sourcebook,

searchable by most fields. It comes with ACT®, a contact management software.   It is available in two versions: professional manager (including 89 catagories of information) and personal manager (containing 16 catagories). See citation: 248.

General Discographies

MUZE.   Quarterly.   Ebsco Publishing/Fulcrum Technologies, Inc. DOS/Mac.

The academic version of the touch-screen kiosk discography marketed to retail record outlets.   It lists CDs and cassettes of all styles of music.   It also lists music videos.   You can search by album title, performer, guest artist, song/work title, composer, subject, and record label.   All search fields can also be searched by keyword with Boolean operators.

Billboard/Phonolog Music Reference Library on CD-ROM. Quarterly.   New York: Billboard Electronic Publishing.   DOS.

A discography of albums, cassettes and CD discs of all styles, including classical.   More than 80,000 titles are included.

Critical Discographies

All Music Guide.   Livonia, MI: Selectware Technologies, CD-ROM for IBM compatibles.   Moraga, CA: Great Bear Technologies, discs for Macintosh.

An electronic version of the book.   Searching is limited to artist or album title.   Searches can be limited by genre.   See citation 352.

Index

Korall, Burt
  Drummin' Men, 173
Korner, Alexis
  Jazz on Record, 353
Kozinn, Allan
  The Guitar, 174
Krasker, Tommy
  Catalog of the American Musical, 71
Krenshaw, Marshall
  Hollywood Rock: A Guide to Rock 'n' Roll in the Movies, 417
Kruglinski, Susan
  Einstein's Guide to the Musical Universe, 250

The L.A. Musical History Tour: A Guide to the Rock and Roll
  Landmarks of Los Angeles, 385
LaBlanc, Michael L., ed.
  Contemporary Musicians, 175
Laing, Dave
  Encyclopedia of Rock, 106
  The Faber Companion to Popular Music, 161
Laing, Ralph
  Jazz Records : The Specialist Labels, 300
Lamb, Andrew
  Ganzl's Book of the Musical Theatre, 415
Landon, Grelun
  Encyclopedia of Folk, Country & Western Music, 206
Language of Commercial Music, 237
The Language of Twentieth Century Music: A Dictionary of Terms, 233
Larkin, Colin
  The Guinness Encyclopedia of Popular Music, 112
Laufenberg, Cindy
  1994 Songwriters Market, 249
Lauferberg, Frank
  Rock and Pop, Day by Day, 397
Laughton, Robert
  Gospel Records: 1943-1969, 288
Lax, Roger
  The Great Song Thesaurus, 72
Leadbitter, Mike
  Blues Records, January 1943 to December 1966, 301
Leder, Jan
  Women in Jazz: A Discography of Instrumentalists, 1913-1968, 302
Lee, Bill (William F.)
  Bill Lee's Jazz Dictionary, 235
  People in Jazz, 176
The Legends of Rock Guitar, 219

LYRICISTS see SONGWRITERS

MacGillivray, Scott
  The Soundies Distributing Corporation of America, 426
Macken, Bob
  The Rock Music Souce Book, 76
Mackenzie, Harry
  Basic Musical Library, "P" Series, 1-1000, 299
  One Night Stand Series, 1-1001, 308
Magee, Jeffrey
  Jazz Standards on Record, 1900-1942 : A Core Repertory, 58
Mapp, Edward
  Directory of Blacks in the Performing Arts, 179
Marco, Guy A.
  Encyclopedia of Recorded Sound in the United States, 113
Markewich, Reese
  Bibliography of Jazz Compositions Based on ... Standard Tunes, 77
Marsh, Dave
  Merry Christmas, Baby, 78
  The Book of Rock Lists, 398
  The Heart of Rock & Soul, 364
The Marshall Cavendish Illustrated History of Popular Music, 98
Mattfeld, Julius
  Variety Music Cavalcade, 79
Mawhinney, Paul C.
  The MusicMaster: The 45 RPM Record Directory, 309
McAleer, Dave
  The All Music Book of Hit Singles, 310
  The Omnibus Book of British and American Hit Singles, 311
McCarthy, Albert
  Jazz on Record: A Critical Guide to the First 50 Years, 365
McCoy, Judy
  Rap Music in the 1980s, 20
McGee, Mark Thomas
  The Rock and Roll Movie Encyclopedia of the 1950s, 420
McGovern, Dennis
  Sing Out, Louise, 180
McRae, Barry
  The Jazz Handbook, 181
Meadows, Eddie S.
  Jazz Reference and Research Materials, 21
Mecklenburg, Carl Gregor Herzog zu
  International Jazz Bibliography, 22
Meeker, David
  Jazz in the Movies, 421
Meeting the Blues, 154

About the Author

GARY HAGGERTY is Assistant Library Director at Berklee College of Music in Boston. He is a specialist in contemporary popular music and is a professional performing musician. He holds degrees in music and library science.